Better Letters

2ND EDITION

A Handbook of Business and Personal Correspondence

Jan Venolia

TEN SPEED PRESS
Berkeley, California

Ten Speed Press
Box 7123
Berkeley, California 94707

Cover design by Fifth Street Design
Interior design by Toni Tajima

Library of Congress Cataloging-in-Publication Data

Venolia, Jan.
    Better letters: Second edition/Jan Venolia.
      p. cm.
    Includes bibliographical references (p.) and index.
    ISBN 0-89815-763-3
    1. Letter writing. 2. Commercial correspondence. I. Title.
  PE1483.V4 1995
  808.6—dc20

95-41194
CIP

Printed in Canada.

First printing second edition, 1995.

2 3 4 5 6 7 8 9 10 — 02 01 00 99 98

Distributed in Australia by Simon & Schuster Australia, in Canada by Publishers Group West, in New Zealand by Tandem Press, in South Africa by Real Books, in Singapore and Malaysia by Berkeley Books, and in the United Kingdom and Europe by Airlift Books.

Business, love, and friendship
all demand a ready pen.
—THE NEW UNIVERSAL LETTER-WRITER, 1850

...or typewriter,

...or computer.

Table of Contents

Are Letters Obsolete? 1

1 Letter-Writing Style 5

Write Clearly
Write Concisely
Write in a Readable Style
Is E-Mail a Special Case?
Are the Rules of Style Unbending?

2 Composing a Better Letter 31

Getting Started
The First Draft
Final Steps

3 The Look of the Letter 47

Letter Placement and Design
Punctuating the Parts of a Business Letter
Business Letter Format
The Elements of a Business Letter
Envelopes

4 Dear Sir or Madam 83

Social Titles and Salutations
Problem Words

5 Some Examples of Business Letters 97

Request for Action
Cover Letter
Sales Letter
Letter of Inquiry
Response to Inquiry
Complaint Letter
Response to Complaint Letter
Business Thank-You Letter
Collection Letter
Job-Related Letters
      Resume Cover Letter
      The Ineffective Cover Letter
      Job Application Letter

Post-Interview Thank-You Letter
Letter of Recommendation
Letter of Resignation

6   Some Examples of Personal Letters **135**

Handwritten or Typed?
Letters to Family and Friends
   Thank-You Notes
   Keeping in Touch
   Travel
   To Your Children
   Sympathy
   Response to a Sympathy Letter
As Consumer and Citizen
   Complaint Letter
   Letter to Government Representative
   Soliciting Funds

Appendix A: Word Choices **153**

Action Verbs
Expressions to Avoid

Appendix B: Postal Service Abbreviations **156**

Two-Letter State and Province Abbreviations
Street Address Abbreviations
Business Word Abbreviations

Appendix C: Forms of Address **161**

Appendix D: Test Yourself **168**

Grammar and Usage
Punctuation and Capitalization
Style
Spelling

Resources for the Letter Writer **182**

Index **185**

Are Letters Obsolete?

The dynamic of the workplace has changed dramatically in recent years. Management-level employees have monitors and keyboards instead of secretaries, inter-office memos fly back and forth via e-mail, and growing numbers of people are telecommuting from a home office.

Have these changes made letters obsolete? Far from it. Written words, whether on a computer screen or on paper, remain essential to business and personal communication. Think of how many ways we still need letters:

- to sell products and services

- to handle routine business

- to establish good will

- to apply for a job

- to respond to or register complaints

- to collect money

- to introduce ourselves to colleagues

- to extend condolences

- to express thanks or send congratulations

In fact, letters are so useful in the business world that people are awash with them. The letter you write competes with dozens of others for your reader's attention. Most of those letters are wordy and dull, however, so your well-crafted letter will stand out.

At first blush, model letters might look like the easy way out. Literally hundreds of pre-written letters "for every occasion" await you on the shelves of libraries and book-stores. These one-size-fits-all letters are even included in the latest word-processing soft-ware; all you have to do is press a few keys and fill in the blanks. Tempting though these canned letters may be, they will never match the spark of originality or the relevance of a letter you write individually. When you write it yourself, you convey the sense that a human being, not a machine, is behind the words—and that means a lot these days.

I have included some sample letters in *Better Letters*, but they are intended as illustra-tions of the principles of good writing, not as models to be shoehorned into your situa-tion. My aim is to equip you to generate your own letters so you won't have to rely on the skill of others.

Here's how I propose to do that. Chapter 1, "Letter-Writing Style," is a quick course in the elements of style: how to write clearly, concisely, and readably. Chapter 2, "Composing a Better Letter," takes you from the first steps in organizing your information through the final tasks of revising and proofing. Chapter 3, "The Look of the Letter," presents options for making your letters appealing to the eye and correctly formatted by modern standards. Chapter 4, "Dear Sir or Madam," suggests some easy ways to remove gender bias from your correspondence. Chapter 5, "Some Examples of Business Letters," and Chapter 6, "Some Examples of Personal Letters", illustrate specific types of correspondence with the aim of stirring up ideas about how to write your own letters.

The appendixes include a variety of aids for the letter writer: lists of action verbs and expressions to avoid, Postal Service abbreviations, forms of address, and some quizzes to sharpen writing skills. And finally, an extended bibliography appears in "Resources for the Letter Writer." Some delightful drawings by Ellen Sasaki and a few light touches in the text should make the process of becoming a better letter writer more enjoyable.

The skills you gain in mastering the art of letter writing will prove handy anytime you are called upon to express yourself. When you can "talk on paper" you are valuable to a company and thus your prospects are brighter. Copies of letters are often circulated to people other than the addressee; if your letter favorably impresses your boss, for example, while making a sale or resolving a complaint, it will have accomplished more than its immediate purpose.

Letters are efficient. They conserve your time and multiply your efforts by allowing you to reach more people than you could meet in person or even contact by telephone. Further, the process of writing a letter gives you an opportunity to refine your ideas, and the recipient of your letter has a chance to mull them over. In contrast, phone calls are intrusive; they demand immediate attention and allow little time for reflection. Letters also have the advantage of leaving a tangible record.

Today's sophisticated equipment enhances your ability to communicate, but it doesn't teach you how to write a good letter. That's where *Better Letters* comes in. Put it to work for you in business and at home.

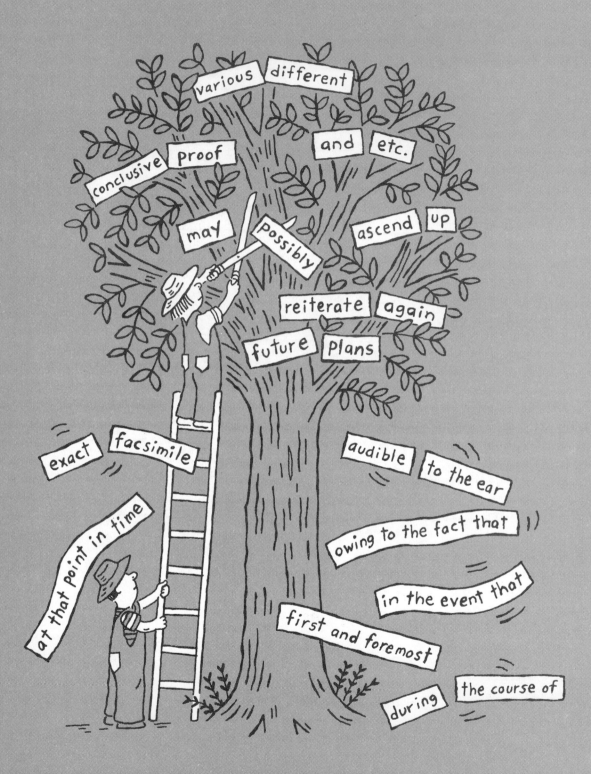

Omit unnecessary words. See page 18.

1 Letter-Writing Style

Write Clearly **6**

Develop a good working relationship
  with words

Use fresh words

Use concrete words

Write with strong verbs

Use short, familiar words

Use the right words

Make your references clear

Avoid misplaced words

Write Concisely **18**

Omit unnecessary words

Use modifiers sparingly

Write in a Readable Style **21**

Write in the active voice

Emphasize important points

Keep sentences short

Avoid a series of monotonous sentences

Use paragraphing to help the reader

Provide road signs for the reader

Is E-Mail a Special Case? **27**

**Are the Rules of
Style Unbending?** **28**

1 Letter-Writing Style

To write well requires a working knowledge of the elements of style. Writing good letters poses an additional challenge: You must quickly win the reader's attention and convey your message. Furthermore, your letter must compete with phone calls, appointments, meetings, and other letters.

To be effective, your letters should be:

Neat. Make a good first impression; the opportunity doesn't come along twice.

Clear. Help your reader understand your message promptly.

Accurate. Build good business relationships by providing precise information.

Prompt. Answer letters at the earliest opportunity; that will encourage your correspondent to do the same and help you look responsible.

Friendly. Stress "you" rather than "I"; show that you understand your reader's situation.

Brief. Don't waste a busy person's time.

Correct. Use words properly; spell and hyphenate them correctly. Look up words you are uncertain about.

Courteous. Include courtesies such as "Thank you" and "Please" even in the briefest letter.

Complete. Don't leave loose ends; provide the necessary information in appropriate detail.

Letter writing is a special kind of writing, directed toward a particular audience for a specific purpose. You may have an audience of one person or of thousands; your reason for writing may be to make money or to keep in touch with friends. Whatever your objective, make your writing style *clear, concise,* and *readable.*

WRITE CLEARLY

People are swamped with information. It comes at them from all directions, often shrouded in a fog of vague, trite words. If your letters generate such fog, you force readers to puzzle through the details to determine whether they are of interest. They may not have the time—or the inclination—to make such an effort. Furthermore, unclear writing reflects unclear thinking, which can damage your credibility.

To keep your letters off of the fast track to the wastebasket, choose the best words to express your ideas, and arrange those words to help the reader grasp your ideas.

◨ **Develop a good relationship with words.** _____

Words are your tools. The more words you have at your command, the more accurately you can convey your ideas. The more effectively you arrange words, the more successful you will be in sending an idea from your mind to your reader's mind.

A word is not a crystal, transparent and unchanged; it is the skin of a living thought and may vary greatly in color and content according to the circumstances and time in which it is used.
—OLIVER WENDELL HOLMES, JR.

Consulting a dictionary as you write can improve your skill with words in many ways. In letter writing, dictionaries are most often used for spelling *(concensus* or *consensus?)* and definitions (What does *colloquial* mean?).

But a good dictionary enhances your word skills in other, less obvious, ways:

- synonyms (*burn, scorch,* and *singe*)

- usage (Is *typo* colloquial?)

- pronunciation (Is *consortium* pronounced *con-sor-tee-um* or *con- sor-shum*?)

- word division (*know-ledge* or *knowl-edge?*)

- word roots (*polyglot:* from Greek *poly* [much, many] + *glotta* [tongue])

The front matter in your dictionary is a cornucopia of interesting information. My edition of *The American Heritage Dictionary* not only tells me how to use the dictionary but has articles on such subjects as grammar and meaning, dialects, usage, and a brief history of the English language. There's even an article on computers in language analysis and lexicography.

Under headings like "Guide to This Dictionary" or "Explanatory Notes," dictionaries provide practical information: a key to phonetic symbols, descriptions of what their labels mean (e.g., Slang, Obsolete, and Rare), and how they indicate preference among spelling variations. The latter is especially important, since dictionaries are so often consulted as the source of correct spellings.

Some variations in spelling are considered equally correct, others less so. Many dictionaries show equally acceptable variations by separating them with a comma or the word *or*.

ax, axe   ax *or* axe

Typically, if one spelling is preferred, the less acceptable variant is listed after the preferred form and is preceded by the word *Also*.

esophagus…*Also*, oesophagus.

Generally, you should choose preferred spellings, so read the front matter in your dictionary to find out how they are indicated.

The dictionary and thesaurus that come with word processors, though handy for spelling and synonyms, are much more limited than a printed dictionary. The bibliography beginning on p. 182 lists some good dictionaries; have one nearby when you write.

Use fresh words.

Writers are often advised to write the way they speak. This suggestion should not be taken literally, since our speech is rambling and full of redundancies. We punctuate sentences with pet words or phrases, like "basically" and "you know," and we rely on gestures and facial expressions to carry our meaning.

A kernel of truth in the write-as-you-speak advice is that you don't speak stilted language, so why write it? Write only words you can imagine yourself actually saying. This will eliminate such sentences as,

"Receipt of yours of August 22 is acknowledged herewith."

Would you ever *say* that to anyone? People used to think a letter wasn't businesslike unless it employed such stuffy terminology, but good business language today is much more direct.

The write-as-you-speak approach may help you if you freeze up when confronted with the need to write. Imagine yourself speaking to the reader and you will produce more naturally flowing prose.

Ready-made phrases are the prefabricated strips of words…that come crowding in when you do not want to take the trouble to think through what you are saying. They will construct your sentences for you—even think your thoughts for you—and at need they will perform the important service of partially concealing your meaning even from yourself.

—GEORGE ORWELL

Constantly ask yourself, "Is there a simpler way to say that?" Be on the lookout for the buzzwords and cliches of the day: words like *bottom line, input, game plan, rocket scie-*

tist, no-win situation, downsize, back burner, and *stonewall.* Challenge yourself to replace them with less overworked words.

Some hackneyed expressions commonly found in letters are listed in Appendix A (p. 154). Look them over to see if you recognize some "ready-made phrases" from your own letters. Revise your writing by using the suggested alternatives or just by deleting the stilted language. Often jargon serves no purpose; remove it and you immediately improve your letter.

Here are some examples of how you might make such changes:

(1) afford an opportunity

The long way to say *allow* or *permit.*

Wordy: A meeting will afford us the opportunity to exchange ideas.

Better: A meeting will allow us to exchange ideas.

(2) feel free to, do not hesitate to

Unnecessarily patronizing. A simple *please* is better.

Poor: Feel free to (do not hesitate to) call me if I can help.

Better: Please call me if I can help.

(3) in the amount of

A relic from bygone days. Modernize by using *for.*

Outmoded: I enclose a check in the amount of $12.50.

Better: I enclose a check for $12.50.

(4) meet with approval

A stiff phrase that uses too many words.

Stiff: If it meets with your approval...

Better: If you approve...

(5) same

An awkward stand-in for something referred to previously.

Rewrite using a pronoun (it, them, etc.) or the name of the item.

Awkward: Your check arrived this morning and thank you for same.

Better: Thank you for the check that arrived this morning.

(6) under separate cover

Another relic that continues to appear in modern letters. Use *separately* or indicate the method of mailing.

Hackneyed: I am sending a copy of the book under separate cover.

Better: I am sending a copy of the book by Special 4th Class mail.

(7) per

Latin words like *per* are often used in order to give writing a legal aura. Striking the word "per" from your vocabulary is probably a good idea, unless you are referring to measurements such as miles per gallon or cost per unit.

Stilted: Per our conversation, I am enclosing a copy of the report.

Better: As we agreed, I am enclosing a copy of the report.

Malcolm Baldrige, a former Secretary of Commerce, worked hard to promote the cause of Plain English in his department. He noticed when he came to Washington that many people spoke in multi-syllabic words and phrases that he wasn't sure even they understood. "There is a kind of protection in statements and recommendations so vague that they can be interpreted two or three ways. That's not communication; that's covering one's flanks."

✎ Use concrete words.

Concrete words are specific and descriptive. They deal with things we can see, hear, smell, touch, and taste: cellular phones, rubber cement, sirens, X-Acto knives, Velcro, leather jackets, and horseradish.

Abstract words—efficiency, danger, speed, heroism—have different meanings for different people. When you write in abstractions and generalities, you increase the risk that your reader won't know what you mean. Vagueness usually takes less effort, but if you wish to convert a flabby style into a crisp one, you will deal in particulars and make your language specific, definite, and concrete.

In the space of one sentence, Charles Dickens' character Mr. Micawber illustrates both an overblown abstraction and its concrete translation:

It is not an avocation of a remunerative description—in other words, it does not pay.

The following examples turn vague statements into more precise ones.

Vague: She is a good worker.

Precise: She introduced changes that cut response time from three days to one.

Vague: Our primary objective is to consider available alternatives in order to determine a viable option for improving working conditions by removing environmental hazards.

Precise: We want to find a way to remove airborne asbestos particles.

Vague: In view of our domestic economic situation...

Precise: With unemployment near seven percent...

Vague: We experienced a marked increase in productivity after management introduced a program to improve the health of our employees.

Precise: The exercise and nutrition program cut absenteeism in half.

Instead of referring to "optimum test results" or "adverse weather conditions," say what the results or conditions were. Your readers will respond more quickly to "35 miles per gallon" or "25 degrees below zero."

Generalities are useful if they help organize or summarize ideas. But when you have climbed into the stratosphere to state a principle, quickly return to sea level with a tangible example. Make concrete words carry your abstract idea. Taking a few moments to clearly convey your meaning costs less than quickly writing an ambiguous letter that requires clarification.

◻ Write with strong verbs.

Letter writing (especially in business) seems to inspire people to bury verbs under nouns and prepositions. Instead of "We discussed...," they write "We held a discussion." The livelier "We agree" is deadened into "We are in agreement." The human touch is harder to detect if it's smothered by such verbiage.

The culprits that invite this smothering are often forms of the verbs *to be, give, have, make,* and *take.* Watch for them, and the other examples below, in your writing.

Change:	To:
arrive at a conclusion	conclude
be in possession	possess
give consideration	consider
have a need	need
have a suspicion	suspect
hold a discussion	discuss
make an adjustment	adjust
make a choice	choose
make a determination	determine
take into consideration	consider

Verbs such as *exist, happen, occur,* and *take place* often contribute to vague, colorless sentences.

Weak: During the strike, tension existed between management and labor.

Stronger: During the strike, tension between management and workers grew.

Weak: A sharp drop occurred in the Dow Jones Industrial Average.

Stronger: The Dow Jones Industrial Average dropped sharply.

A list of strong verbs appears in Appendix A (p. 153).

✐ Use short, familiar words.

Vivid words tend to be short ones, like those we use in everyday speech. When your words are familiar to your reader, you improve the odds of being understood. Choose words like *begin, move,* and *use* rather than *initiate, relocate,* and *utilize.*

Author Gelett Burgess wrote an eight-page essay of one-syllable words. Here is an excerpt:

> *If we use long words too much, we are apt to talk in ruts and use the same old worn ways of speech....Short words are bold. They say just what they mean. They do not leave you in doubt. They are clear and sharp, like signs cut in rock.*

Caution: If you use a shortened version of a word (e.g., *fax* or *demo*), be sure that such informal terminology is suitable and that the way you have used it doesn't create confusion for the reader. The word *fax* has moved quickly into mainstream usage; many people don't even recognize it as a shortened version of *facsimile* and would not be puzzled by different forms of the word (*faxed* or *faxing*). But *demo* would be considered slang, and grammatical variations of the word can baffle the reader. I know, because I was brought to a halt when I encountered the following sentence:

Poor: Demoing boosted CD-ROM sales.

Better: Demonstrations boosted CD-ROM sales.

▣ Use the right words. _____

Know when to write *compliment* and when to write *complement*. Avoid confusing *affect* with *effect*, *principal* with *principle*, *alternate* with *alternative*. I recently received a letter that suggested ways "to elevate the problem." Although there may be occasions when we want to elevate a problem, we more often want to *alleviate* it.

Such errors probably occur because we *hear* words more than we *see* them; differences between words are sometimes hard to pick up by ear. Add to that the frequent misuse of words on radio and television, and you find wrong words going forth and multiplying.

Reading and dictionary use are effective antidotes. Keep a dictionary nearby when you read, and notice how good writers use words. If you are unsure of the meaning of any words or how they should be used, take the few seconds needed to look them up.

Here are some commonly misused pairs of words:

Affect is a verb meaning to have an influence on; *effect* is most commonly used as a noun meaning result or consequence, but it is also a verb meaning to bring about.

New employees are not affected by the ruling. (verb)

The effect of the ruling is limited. (noun)

To effect improved customer relations, we shortened our response time. (verb)

Alternate refers to every other one; *alternative* is a choice.

One alternative is to meet on alternate Tuesdays.

Complement means to complete a whole or satisfy a need; *compliment* means praise.

His skill at baking pies complemented her talent with cakes.

A bake shop customer complimented them on their teamwork.

Continual means over and over again; *continuous* means uninterrupted or unbroken.

Since he coughed continually, the doctor kept him under continuous observation.

Criterion describes a standard or rule on which a decision or judgment is based; *criteria* is the plural form and should not be used as a singular word.

Wrong: a criteria

The criteria is ...

The only criteria ...

Right: a criterion

The criteria are ...

The only criterion ...

Fewer is used for number, especially when referring to individual numbers or units; *less* is used for quantity, as in periods of time, sums of money, or measures of weight or distance.

Automation requires more machines and fewer people.

It would be nice to earn more money in less time.

The dietician recommended eating fewer candy bars and drinking less coffee.

Incorrect use of words suggests sloppy thinking and generally careless work. *Write Right!* contains a longer list of abused words to help you make the right choice. (See "Resources for the Letter Writer," p. 182.)

▧ Make your references clear. _____

Your meaning may be perfectly apparent to you—after all, you wrote the letter. But if you make unclear references, you may mislead or confuse readers. Words like *who*, *which*, *that*, and *it* refer to the preceding noun; if the preceding noun is not the word you intend to refer to, or if too many words come between the noun and its referent, you should rewrite. Here are some ways to make your references clear.

1. Rearrange the words.

> **Confusing:** The senator proposed an amendment to the administration tax bill *which* was opposed by the steel manufacturers.

(Which was opposed, the amendment or the tax bill?)

> **Clear:** The steel manufacturers opposed the senator's amendment to the administration tax bill.

> **Confusing:** The wife of my partner, *who* died recently...

(Who died, the wife or the partner?)

> **Clear:** My partner's wife died recently.

2. Avoid pronouns that have no clear referent.

> **Vague:** The stockholders alleged fraud and mismanagement in the handling of corporate funds, dating back to when *it* was run by...

(What does *it* refer to? *The corporation*, which does not appear as such in the sentence.)

> **Clear:** The stockholders alleged fraud and mismanagement in the handling of funds, dating back to when the corporation was run by...

3. Break up long sentences.

Confusing: The information in this report, *which* has not been available previously because of proprietary considerations, remains confidential and should be filed in a secure place.

(Was the report or the information proprietary?)

Clear: This confidential report contains proprietary information that was not previously available. Please file the report in a secure place.

4. Keep subject and verb together.

Poor: Members of the Board of Directors, who are elected by district each November to serve four-year staggered terms and whose duties require attendance at only one meeting per week, are not eligible for pensions under the city charter.

(Too much ancillary information comes between subject and verb.)

Better: Members of the Board of Directors are not eligible for pensions under the city charter, since they attend only one meeting per week. They are elected by district each November to serve four-year staggered terms.

5. Avoid unintended meanings.

Some sentences are grammatically correct but nonetheless provide a laugh. Rewrite to avoid such situations.

Poor: If the children do not like raw vegetables, boil them.

Better: Boil the vegetables if the children do not like to eat them raw.

Poor: This afternoon there will be meetings in the south and north ends of the church; children will be baptized at both ends.

Better: ...; children will be baptized at both locations.

Poor: Ladies of the church have cast off clothing of every kind; they can be seen in the basement on Friday afternoons.

Better: Ladies of the church have a variety of cast-off clothing available for purchase; the clothing can be seen on Friday afternoons in the basement.

▢ Avoid misplaced words. _____

A *squinting modifier*, as that delightfully descriptive term suggests, is a modifier that points in both directions; one isn't sure whether it refers to the word before or after the modifier.

> **Confusing:** Straight answers must be given to them both in writing and in personal meetings.

Does *both* squint forward or backward in that sentence? The ambiguity disappears when you rewrite.

> **Better:** Straight answers must be given to both of them in writing and in personal meetings.

or

> They must be given straight answers both in writing and in personal meetings.

Placement of the word *only* affects its meaning. Consider the following sentences:

> She told only the affected workers about the layoffs.
>
> She told the affected workers only about the layoffs.

Each has a different meaning. Be sure you said what you intended when you use the word *only*.

Dangling and *misplaced modifiers* can also confuse readers and occasionally give them a laugh—at your expense.

Dangling Modifiers:

In a liquid, we observe the molecules to be easily agitated.

Hanging from the flagpole, he saw his country's flag.

Corrected:

We observe the molecules to be easily agitated when they are in a liquid.

He saw his country's flag hanging from the flagpole.

Misplaced Modifiers:

The owner of the Ferrari is a distinguished-looking gentleman with a Van Dyke beard named Marshall Myers.

If you do not have a vehicle in which to store your food, please ask for help in properly hanging it from a Park Ranger.

Corrected:

The owner of the Ferrari, Marshall Myers, is a distinguished-looking gentleman with a Van Dyke beard.

If you do not have a vehicle in which to store your food, please ask a Park Ranger for help in hanging it properly.

WRITE CONCISELY

The most valuable of all talents is that of never using two words when one will do.

—THOMAS JEFFERSON

We often use not just two but several words where one would do. Your readers are probably as busy as you are; don't make them work too hard.

◩ Omit unnecessary words.

Remove padding when you revise a rough draft, leaving only the words that are essential to your meaning.

Roundabout	Direct
in view of the fact that	
owing to the fact that	because
due to the fact that	
in spite of the fact that	although
the fact that we arrived late	our late arrival
some questions relating to this issue	some relevant questions
in compliance with your request	at your request
the majority of	most
It is our hope that	We hope that

Cut doubles in half, such as *first and foremost, unless and until*. Many of these redundant expressions have the added drawback of being cliches. In the following examples, the italicized words can be deleted with no loss.

Submission of entries must be timely *and punctual.*

We wish to express our appreciation *and gratitude.*

Unless *and until* we hear from you, ...

I will repeat these instructions *again* at the end of the session.

We cannot approve of the changes in any way, *shape, or form.*

Delete empty phrases like *consideration should be given to, you can appreciate that, in this connection,* and *it is a matter of prime importance.* Such padding contributes nothing to your meaning. Similarly, phrases like *unsubstantiated rumor* and *growing groundswell* are not only empty but nonsensical. A rumor that was substantiated would cease to be a rumor. Watch for and trim such expressions.

Rewrite most sentences to avoid the phrases *there is* and *there are.*

Wordy: There are several companies that are qualified to do the work.

Better: Several companies are qualified to do the work.

Sometimes you can replace the forms of the verb *to be* (*is, are*) with action verbs.

Wordy: Throughout the day, there was an atmosphere of increasing excitement.

Better: Throughout the day, excitement mounted.

Wherever suitable, compress clauses beginning with *which, that,* or *who* into fewer words.

Wordy: The senator, *who* comes from Ohio, gave a speech *that* was long and tedious.

Better: The senator from Ohio gave a long, tedious speech.

Wordy: Which are the ones that get your attention?

Better: Which ones get your attention?

Wordy: The board meeting, *which* lasted two hours, was followed by a press conference.

Better: The two-hour board meeting was followed by a press conference.

or

A press conference followed the two-hour board meeting.

Your readers will appreciate the vigor of your writing if you eliminate wordiness.

Replace:	with:
and etc.	etc.
at all times	always
at a time when	when
at that point in time	then
at this point in time	now
blue in color	blue
conclusive proof	proof
consensus of opinion	consensus
deeds and actions	(Use one or the other)
during the course of	during
end result	result
exactly identical	identical
exact same	(Use one or the other)
few in number	few
final outcome	outcome
for the period of one year	for one year
future plans	plans
great majority	majority
have a belief in	believe
if and when	(Use one or the other)
important essentials	essentials
in the vast majority of cases	in most cases
my personal opinion	my opinion *or* I believe that
new initiative	initiative
on a monthly basis	monthly
perhaps you might like	perhaps you would like *or* you might like
positive identification	identification
reduce to a minimum	minimize
refer back to	refer to
reiterate again	reiterate
round in shape	round
streamlined in appearance	streamlined
true facts	facts
until such time as	until
various different	(Use one or the other)
very necessary	necessary

✐ Use modifiers sparingly. _____

Vigorous adjectives and adverbs strengthen your meaning.

baffling instructions	tardy response
lively debate	lucid argument
emphatic statement	faulty reasoning
timely proposal	hauntingly familiar
acrid smoke	unforgiving deadline

Overused modifiers, on the other hand, make your writing stale.

richly deserved	absolute necessity
eminently qualified	bitter end
perfectly clear	checkered career
acid test	final analysis

When you are tempted to prop up a word with an adjective or adverb, consider whether the word by itself might be stronger.

Poor: His response was quick and very emphatic.

Better: His response was quick and emphatic.

Poor: Your vote in this matter is truly crucial.

Better: Your vote in this matter is crucial.

Vigorous writing is concise. A sentence should contain no unnecessary words, a paragraph no unnecessary sentences, for the same reason that a drawing should have no unnecessary lines and a machine no unnecessary parts.

—WILLIAM STRUNK, JR.

WRITE IN A READABLE STYLE

When you write in a readable style, you show that you are aware of your audience and concerned about your reader's interests. Conversely, a readable style communicates your own humanity. In the world of automated tellers and answering machines, a human tone is welcome. The following pages suggest a few ways to improve the readability of your writing.

✎ Write in the active voice. _____

When you write in the active voice, the subject of the sentence *performs* the action:

> Man bites dog.
>
> The committee read your report.

When you use the passive voice, the subject *receives* the action.

> Dog bitten by man.
>
> Your report was read by the committee.

The active voice is more forceful and direct—and often requires fewer words. The passive voice tends to encourage anonymity; reports are written, actions are taken, and suggestions are made by some nameless source.

The passive voice combines a form of the verb *to be* with a past participle: *was read, have been sold, were reported, had been opened, will have been seen.* Become expert at sniffing out passive constructions and converting them into the active form.

> **Passive:** A feasibility study was conducted by the marketing staff.
>
> **Active:** The marketing staff conducted a feasibility study.

> **Passive:** Revisions of the charter have been made to remove outdated provisions.
>
> **Active:** We have revised the charter to remove outdated provisions.

The following sentence shifts from active to passive:

> When the sales representatives completed their reports, the data were analyzed and a marketing plan was outlined by the head of each department.

Here it is, rewritten entirely in the active voice:

> When the sales representatives completed their reports, the head of each department analyzed the data and outlined a marketing plan.

The passive voice is appropriate when the recipient of the action is more important than the performer of the action.

> The pedestrian was struck by a car.
>
> The records were lost by a careless employee.

Do not use the passive voice to avoid saying "I" or "we."

> **Poor:** It is recommended by this office...
>
> **Better:** We recommend...

◻ Emphasize important points.

Put more important ideas in the main clause of a sentence, and less important details in subordinate clauses or phrases. (A main clause could stand alone as a separate sentence; subordinate clauses are fragments that do not express a complete thought.) For example:

> As you may know, we make a routine credit check before opening a new account.

> In view of the number of books your company orders each week, you will be interested in our new volume discounts.

The clauses "we make a routine credit check..." and "you will be interested..." carry the main ideas. The remaining information is appropriately given less emphasis by being placed in subordinate clauses.

Someone who is skimming will pause at first words and first lines. Thus, you increase your emphasis by putting the main clause at the beginning of the sentence or paragraph.

> Please return the proofs promptly; the printer's deadline is October 1.

You may instead wish to build to a climax by moving from simple to complicated, less important to more important, and so on.

> The firestorm destroyed trees, homes—entire blocks.

> *I dislike arguments of any kind. They are always vulgar, and often convincing.*
>
> —OSCAR WILDE

Don't bury your climax in the middle of the sentence.

> **Weak:** Our investment in research has finally led to a cure for the common cold, after years of experimentation and unproductive effort.

> **Strong:** After years of tracking down promising leads only to find ourselves in blind alleys, our research has finally paid off with a cure for the common cold.

Inverting the customary order is another way to achieve emphasis.

Right you are!

Seldom did he manage to finish on time.

Use bullets and lists to bring selected material to the reader's attention. This technique conveys information more easily than a paragraph of text.

Poor: We need the following information in order to complete your application: your address and telephone number, date and place of birth, social security number, current employer, and three credit references.

Better: We need the following information in order to complete your application:

1. address

2. telephone number

3. date of birth

4. place of birth

5. social security number

6. current employer

7. three credit references

When itemizing, use a parallel form for all items. If the first item is a complete sentence, make all other items complete sentences; if the first item begins with an action verb, begin all items with action verbs. Don't mix phrases, sentences, commands, and nouns in one list.

Wrong:

1. Bring your camera.

2. A supply of film.

3. Wear sunglasses.

4. Being on time is important.

Right:

1. Bring your camera and a supply of film.

2. Wear sunglasses.

3. Be on time.

Humor writer Dave Barry offers this advice on adding emphasis:

Q: How is "irregardless" used?
A: It is used to add emphasis to a statement.

Weak: Webster gonna bust your head.
Stronger: Webster gonna bust your head irregardless.

—from "Ask Mr. Language Person"

✎ Keep sentences short.

Good modern writing employs short sentences. A sentence of more than 20 words is often hard to understand, and evidence indicates that readers prefer short sentences.

Long sentences usually result from our failure to *think* before writing. We plunge into a sentence with an idea and then stumble along, adding exceptions, qualifiers, and incidental remarks. We create a verbal maze for our readers.

Perhaps the problem stems from school days when we were taught that each sentence must express a complete thought. As soon as we state an idea, we realize that it isn't complete without some background information or qualifying remarks. Our original idea may branch in several directions, and our "complete thought" becomes bogged down by its own weight.

Coherence may be a better criterion in shaping sentences. Let the words between two periods express a unified idea—but not everything there is to say about a given subject. The following example crowds too many ideas into one sentence; break such sentences in two.

Poor: Today we shipped your order of January 10, and you should be receiving it next week, but since you are a new customer I wanted you to know that we allow an additional discount of 3% if you make your payment within 10 days.

Better: Your order of January 10 was shipped today and should arrive next week. As a new customer, you may not be aware that we allow an additional 3% discount for payment received within 10 days.

Sometimes you have to rewrite one sentence as several to make it more manageable.

Poor: I regret to report that a severe winter storm closed our factory and disrupted delivery of two critical components, making your shipment two weeks late, but we have now received all the necessary parts and our crew is working overtime to put production back on schedule.

Better: I am sorry to report that your shipment will be two weeks late. The winter storm that closed our factory also delayed delivery of two critical components. However, we now have all the necessary parts and expect to be back on schedule soon.

A sentence should read as if its author, had he held a plough instead of a pen, could have drawn a furrow deep and straight to the end.

—Henry David Thoreau

⊡ Avoid a series of monotonous sentences. _____

A short, punchy sentence loses its punchiness when it's in a string of short, punchy sentences. A group of subject-verb-object sentences is not only boring to read but gives equal weight to every detail, suggesting that you have not evaluated your ideas. By varying sentence length and pattern, you avoid a deadening sameness.

> Thank you for your letter of March 9. Our production department is looking into the problem you described. They will report their findings within a week. We will advise you of the results of their investigation. We appreciate your telling us about the problem.

Long, complicated sentence after long, complicated sentence can be equally tedious for the reader.

> Thank you for your letter of March 9 in which you describe a type of problem we had never encountered before and which we are grateful for your having brought to our attention. Our production department is seeking a solution, which we are confident they will find, and we will report the results of their research within a week. As soon as we have their report, we will notify you of their findings in the hope that their solution will apply to your situation.

Soften the abrupt sentences of the first example by adding introductory phrases and sorting some of the ideas into more-important and less-important clauses. Provide relief from the long-winded sentences in the second example by breaking some of them into smaller units. The result might be something like this:

> The problem you described in your letter of March 9 is one we have never encountered. As soon as our production department finds a solution—probably within a week—we will notify you. We appreciate your having taken the time to write us.

⊡ Use paragraphing to help the reader. _____

Solid pages of type are formidable. By grouping sentences into readable units, you can provide spacing that gives the page a more pleasing appearance and makes your ideas more accessible.

The "topic sentence," which carries the main idea of a paragraph, may be placed at the beginning or end of the paragraph. The other sentences in the paragraph relate to this key sentence, expanding or illustrating its thesis.

Look for natural ways to group ideas. Do not jar the reader by arbitrarily separating two sentences that obviously belong together. Although you should break an overly long paragraph in two, do not combine two small paragraphs if they deal with different subjects.

Long paragraphs are difficult to follow; on the other hand, a letter consisting entirely of short paragraphs gives a breathless, hiccuppy impression. The occasional one-sentence paragraph is good for emphasis, but a letter of nothing but one-sentence paragraphs suggests a lazy writer. Take the time to figure out which sentences should be grouped into paragraphs.

Proper paragraphing allows you to draw attention to certain points or to change the subject. Reserve short paragraphs for the points you want to emphasize. See your paragraphs not as isolated units but as coordinated parts of the whole, with each paragraph creating a unified impression and contributing to the smooth flow of ideas. This will develop more easily if you work from a logical outline.

▯ Provide road signs for the reader. _____

Use words and phrases to bring the reader along with you. For example,

> —to signal the direction you are taking:
>
> > *To explain the concept briefly,*
> >
> > *Best of all,*
> >
> > *As I mentioned on the phone...*

> —to indicate a change of course:
>
> > *However,*
> >
> > *Despite this,*
> >
> > *In contrast,*
> >
> > *On the other hand,*

> —to stress important points:
>
> > *Here's the key to the whole program:*
> >
> > *Now, for the most exciting development...*
> >
> > *By acting now...*

The more road signs you provide for the reader, the greater the likelihood that you will both arrive at the same destination.

IS E-MAIL A SPECIAL CASE?

E-mail is usually a more informal type of correspondence than letters that are printed and sent by traditional methods. It is heavily used for interoffice memos, many of which are never printed out but are only stored in computer files.

E-mail presents some attractive advantages. The informality and speed of e-mail are a large part of its usefulness. When an idea occurs to you that you want to pass on to your counterpart in another branch, you can type your message and it is sent, received, read, and filed—all in a matter of moments. Obviously, this kind of communication doesn't call for a lot of planning and reworking, as long as your message is understandable.

Another advantage is that you can copy text from incoming e-mail without retyping and then paste it into new correspondence; this makes it easy to pass the text along to a new recipient or to respond to the sender, point by point. With the click of a mouse, you can attach an entire document to outgoing e-mail. And you can send one letter to a long list of people in an instant.

But there are temptations involved in e-mail that are best avoided. When all you have to do to transmit a letter is type it and click "Send," it is easy to fire off half-baked ideas. Before sending e-mail, pause and ask yourself if you are being hasty. Will your memo or letter produce snickers or contribute to an escalating flame war? Would you want to disown it a day or a week later?

The most attractive features of e-mail—its speed and interactive nature—almost invite knee-jerk responses and verbosity. Avoid wasting people's time and computer memory with irrelevant thoughts, unclear proposals, offensive implications, and an abundance of typos.

To answer the opening question, e-mail is a special case in that it provides new opportunities and new hazards. Its speed requires the exercise of even greater caution than in general correspondence. However, in e-mail as in any other form of written communication, the need for good writing remains.

Are the Rules of Style Unbending?

Letters that are clear, concise, and readable will generally follow the rules presented in this chapter. But rules are only guides for most situations. You needn't always write with short words, short sentences, and the active voice. If you know the rules, you can decide when it's suitable to break them. In doing so, you will be acting from knowledge, not ignorance. As you develop your writing skills, all of your correspondence—from quickly dashed-off e-mail to the carefully crafted proposal—will benefit.

Break any of these rules sooner than say anything outright barbarous.
—George Orwell

I once received a letter that violated many of the rules of letter writing in the space of three sentences. The letter appears on the following page, edited only to protect the guilty.

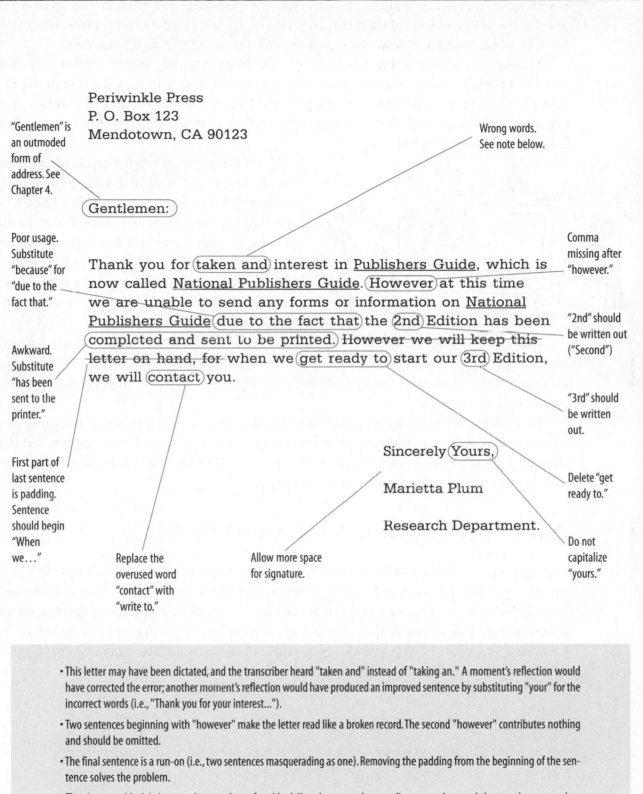

Periwinkle Press
P. O. Box 123
Mendotown, CA 90123

"Gentlemen" is an outmoded form of address. See Chapter 4.

Gentlemen:

Wrong words. See note below.

Poor usage. Substitute "because" for "due to the fact that."

Thank you for taken and interest in Publishers Guide, which is now called National Publishers Guide. However at this time we are unable to send any forms or information on National Publishers Guide due to the fact that the 2nd Edition has been completed and sent to be printed. However we will keep this letter on hand, for when we get ready to start our 3rd Edition, we will contact you.

Comma missing after "however."

Awkward. Substitute "has been sent to the printer."

"2nd" should be written out ("Second")

"3rd" should be written out.

First part of last sentence is padding. Sentence should begin "When we…"

Sincerely Yours,

Marietta Plum

Research Department.

Delete "get ready to."

Do not capitalize "yours."

Replace the overused word "contact" with "write to."

Allow more space for signature.

- This letter may have been dictated, and the transcriber heard "taken and" instead of "taking an." A moment's reflection would have corrected the error; another moment's reflection would have produced an improved sentence by substituting "your" for the incorrect words (i.e., "Thank you for your interest…").
- Two sentences beginning with "however" make the letter read like a broken record. The second "however" contributes nothing and should be omitted.
- The final sentence is a run-on (i.e., two sentences masquerading as one). Removing the padding from the beginning of the sentence solves the problem.
- The signature block is incorrectly spaced; put four blank lines between the complimentary close and the typed name, and no blank lines between the typed name and "Research Department."

Step into your reader's shoes. See page 36.

2 Composing a Better Letter

Getting Started **32**

Brainstorm on paper

Work from an outline

Step into your reader's shoes

Choose a suitable tone

The First Draft **38**

Arouse interest with your
    opening paragraph

Make your letter the right length

Leave a good impression with
    your closing paragraph

Final Steps **43**

Revising

Proofreading

2 Composing a Better Letter

The preceding rules of style may at first be a bit daunting. For the moment, put them aside. At this point, you want to write freely, focusing on the material to be covered in your letter rather than worrying about such matters as the passive voice.

Reflect for a few moments on why you are writing a given letter. What are you trying to accomplish? Complete the sentence that begins, "The reason I am writing this letter is...." Your response might look something like the following:

- to request a job interview

- to explain why I am unable to waive our late-payment penalty

- to express appreciation for an exceptional effort in meeting a deadline

- to request information about applicable regulations

A further question you could ask yourself: "If my letter gets the desired result, my reader will...." Your answer could be anything from "settle an overdue account" to "get a warm feeling from being complimented."

The following pages suggest some steps toward composing a better letter: how to organize information, analyze the reader, write opening and closing paragraphs, and revise drafts. The skills you develop will carry over from one letter to the next, making the task easier as you go along.

GETTING STARTED

◻ Brainstorm on paper.

A good way to begin is to jot down, in no particular order, everything that comes to mind about the letter you want to write. The "jotting" can be done on a computer or by hand. Subjects to be covered, your goal in writing, the tone you want to adopt, anecdotes or sales points—write them all down. Use these notes as insurance that your final letter covers all that you intended.

If you're using a computer, you can easily play around with words and phrases from your notes, experimenting with different combinations and sequences. Try creating topic sentences to state the main idea of each paragraph.

◻ Work from an outline.

Next, draw upon your jottings to create an outline. An outline forces you to think about the specific reasons for writing a letter and how you will go about implementing them.

The more carefully you develop and refine an outline, the more readily the letter will flow when you start writing it.

Some people think an outline is unnecessary—that it is better to start writing the actual letter and make changes in the rough draft. The chief drawback to this approach is that it is harder to revise a draft than an outline, even on a word processor. You can shuffle ideas around more readily when they haven't yet become embedded in complete sentences within paragraphs. Furthermore, you will probably be more willing to make changes when you haven't already put so much time into preparing the first draft.

Computer software can help you structure an outline, allowing you to determine what treatment you want for each heading and sub-heading (e.g., numbered, indented, boldface, with bullets, and so on). The software will not help you decide how to organize the material in outline form, however.

For a simple letter, an outline might consist of a mental list of subjects to be covered. Or you could make notes in the margin of a letter you are answering to indicate how you want to respond: "Thanks, but no thanks," or "Request formal proposal for ad campaign."

If you are thoroughly familiar with the subject of your letter, some key words will probably be all that's needed to summon up ideas about each topic. For example:

Quality Assurance Program

some case histories

reject ratio

cost (incl. insurance)

alternatives

govt. regs.

recommendations

33

A slightly more elaborate outline might look like this:

1. Acknowledge customer's request for waiver of late-payment penalty

   —frustration of "first-time offender"

   —record of timely payments

2. Put problem in perspective

   —10-day grace period allowed

   —difficulties created by making exceptions

   —interest rates, inflation, cash flow

3. Sympathetic "no"

As the subject matter or objectives of the letter become more complex, make your outline more detailed. For example:

1. List the general topics to be covered, using a 3x5 card for each one or following the steps for outlining in your word processing software. For now, assume that each topic will be a paragraph, but don't worry about their order yet.

2. Under each topic enter key words, examples, or facts that will help you remember what you want to write.

3. Determine the order of the items within each topic and mark them accordingly. Place the more important material at the beginning or end of the paragraph, since those places most easily attract the reader's eye. Does the reader need certain information in order to understand what follows? If so, put that information first. If a topic appears to include too many sub-topics, break it into more than one topic.

4. Review your outline for its relevance to your purpose in sending the letter. Is any of your information irrelevant or unnecessary? Is there enough evidence to support your conclusions? If necessary, revise your outline to keep yourself on track.

5. Finally, number the paragraphs or arrange the cards in the order in which you want to present your ideas. Do you want to start with your central thought or statement and then buttress it with discussion and examination? Or would you prefer to build to a climax by identifying a question or issue, discussing it, and finally presenting your conclusions? You might choose a chronological or narrative arrangement in which you discuss events in the order of their occurrence or answer questions in the order in which they were raised. Arrange the cards or text on the monitor accordingly, and start writing.

Long, important letters almost demand extensive outlining. The following example was written for an in-house memo addressed to ABC Company's sales force.

1. Introduction

    a. product long awaited, extensive R&D conducted

    b. importance in ABC's product line

    c. timing of entry into new market

2. Description of Gadgetron

    a. dimensions, power requirements, etc.

    b. features & capabilities: "user friendly"

    c. prices of basic models, options (enclose price list)

3. Test market results

    a. consumer acceptance; modifications made in response to consumer input

    b. competition/our competitive edge

4. Timing of national advertising campaign

    a. TV-radio spots

    b. display ads

    c. billboards (locations)

5. Sales incentive program

    a. regional contests, no. of winners

    b. description of prizes

    c. additional $ for best promotional idea

6. Closing

    a. reminder to take advantage of natl. publicity for sales of related ABC products (Widgetron, Maxitron)

    b. Ads don't make sales—they just get customers ready. It's up to us!

Outlining is a tool for organizing your information, not an end in itself. Don't start with roman numeral I and march down the page with tidy numbered indentations just to meet a formal definition of an outline. Instead, use an outline to arrange information in the most effective sequence and to make sure that nothing has been omitted.

✒ Step into your reader's shoes.

Imagine yourself *talking* to the reader about the material to be covered by your letter. What do you know about him or her that would help you organize your material? Despite differences in age, gender, and occupation, human beings are often motivated by similar interests and concerns. Which ones are you appealing to?

> Time
>
> Money
>
> Love
>
> Health
>
> Safety
>
> Comfort
>
> Prestige
>
> Appearance
>
> Pleasure
>
> Loyalty
>
> Concern about the Environment

Visualize the recipient of a letter and create your own list of motivators. Then write in such a way that you show your understanding of your reader's interests and concerns.

Numerous formulas have been devised to help letter writers focus on the key elements of a letter. Here's one:

> —Occasion (why you're writing)
>
> —Facts (information needed to convert casual interest into specific action)
>
> —Action (a request, suggestion, statement, or demand)
>
> —Closing (courtesy, an offer of additional help or information)

A popular formula for sales letters is AIDA, an acronym for

> —Attention (catching the reader's eye)
>
> —Interest (arousing the reader's interest in what you're writing)
>
> —Desire (making the reader want what you're selling)
>
> —Action (showing the reader how to obtain it)

Letter formulas can help organize your thoughts before writing, or they can be a check for completeness or appropriateness of tone once you've written the letter. But they are just one approach and should never be followed slavishly.

You are your own best "expert" when it comes to knowing what makes a letter effective. Consider what works with you. Among the many letters you receive, which ones get your attention? Which ones move you to action? How did they do it? In contrast, which ones are quickly "round-filed"? Can you learn from them as well? You probably have no better guide to composing your letters.

☝ Choose a suitable tone. _____

The nature of your letter—and your audience—should determine its tone. Obviously the casual, informal letter you write to a close friend would not be suitable for someone you've never met, and vice versa. An unsolicited letter needs to be more persuasive than one written in response to an inquiry or request. A conciliatory tone would be appropriate for a letter written in response to a complaint. Match your tone to the recipient and the occasion.

Some authorities tell you to address the reader by name in the body of a business letter to establish a friendly tone. I question that advice. I react negatively to this kind of "chummy" approach (especially when my name is misspelled), and I may not be unusual in this respect. Perhaps this is another area where you should be guided by your own reactions.

It *is* usually appropriate, however, to let your humanity show through. Choose words that convey your appreciation, regret, optimism, or outrage. If a letter is designed to persuade someone to grant you a job interview or to sell a product, reach out with strong action verbs. Words like *convinced, overhauled,* and *strengthened* convey a vigorous tone.

Weak: I was responsible for changing work assignments to improve productivity.

Strong: I designed a team approach to R&D that enabled us to take on more problems and devise more solutions than the old system of individual responsibility.

Negative or "iffy" words such as *we hope, you may,* or *I trust* convey uncertainty or weakness.

Weak: If you would like to receive a free copy of *Parenting Problems,* just return the enclosed postcard.

Strong: For your free copy of *Parenting Problems,* return the enclosed postcard.

Avoid words that belittle your reader:

You *failed* to make a timely payment,

Your *claim* that ...

As an *infrequent* buyer of our services...

The same message can be sent less antagonistically:

We received your payment three weeks after the final date for payment without penalty.

Your statement that ...

We value every customer, even those we only hear from every few years.

A letter to someone for whom English is a second language calls for a formal, respectful tone. You achieve this by adopting what would seem like excessive formality if you were writing to someone raised in the U.S., but anything less runs the risk of being disrespectful. Avoid contractions, slang, and shortened words; assume that your words will be taken literally. Mary A. DeVries provides helpful suggestions for avoiding the pitfalls of global communication in her excellent book, *Internationally Yours*. (See "Resources for the Letter Writer," p. 182.)

Poor: Thanks for your speedy response to our fax. Let's get busy and settle on a date for a demo.

Better: Thank you for responding quickly to our communication. I suggest that we choose a mutually convenient date for a demonstration.

THE FIRST DRAFT

Write for people who skim. Busy readers check out the first and last paragraphs and any bullets or highlighted parts. If what they see interests them, they go back and read more carefully.

Here's how Dave Barry adds interest:

Tip for Professional Writers: A good way to make your writing more interesting is to include shocking revelations about famous celebrities.

Wrong: "Apply the lacquer with smooth, even strokes."

Right: "Apply the lacquer with smooth, even strokes, bearing in mind that until 1985 Madonna was, biologically, a man."

—from "Ask Mr. Language Person"

▣ Arouse interest with your opening paragraph. _____

The first job of your letter is to engage the reader's attention. You accomplish this by making a good visual impression and by developing interest with your opening paragraph. If you're writing to report that the recipient has won a million-dollar sweepstakes, you will have no trouble. Most business correspondence, however, calls for some degree of salesmanship.

In many cases, you should plunge right in with your reason for writing. Abraham Lincoln didn't mince words when responding to his brother-in-law:

> Your request for eighty dollars, I do not think it best to comply with now.

Don't weigh down the beginning of your letter with repetition of detail that is known; just go straight to the information your correspondent is looking for.

> **Poor:** We have received your letter of February 12 in which you state that the order for 100 copies of *Better Letters* which you placed by telephone on January 30 and which was to be shipped by C&M Trucking has not been received as of the date of writing.
>
> **Better:** I have just checked with our shipping clerk and verified that your order for 100 copies of *Better Letters* was shipped on February 15.

> **Poor:** Replying to your October 16 communication, please accept our apologies for any inconvenience caused by the mistake we made in filling your last purchase order.
>
> **Better:** Thank you for your October 16 letter pointing out our mistake in filling your last order.

Participles (the *-ing* form of a verb) are weak openers.

> Replying to your letter, ...
>
> Knowing of your interest in water polo, ...

Readers want to know quickly why you are writing; participial phrases seem like stalling tactics.

Become a collector of interesting facts. If you keep a file of quotations, word origins, curious statistics, and other stray bits of information, you may find ways to turn them into openings or weave them into the body of your letters. I recently received a letter that opened with a compelling statistic.

> Enough food is produced in the world to meet the nutritional needs of every child, woman, and man. But every day, *34,000 young children die* from malnutrition and disease.

I had to read on. (The letter asked for a contribution to an international relief organization.)

Have you tried beginning a sales letter with a question? Here's one from my file of letters that hooked me:

> What do tennis balls and our mailing lists have in common?

I wanted to know, so again, I read on. (The answer was that the price of both is the same as it was ten years ago.) Here are some other opening questions:

> Do you want to avoid a tax audit?
>
> How long has it been since you had some free time?
>
> Are you ready to trade in your commute for an office in your home?

Look over some of your old letters; see if you can add interest by phrasing the first sentence as a question.

Another example from my files illustrates the hazards of a poorly worded question. The letter began as follows:

> Do you like the idea of saving money and convenient equal monthly payments?

My reaction was that I especially like the idea of saving those convenient equal monthly payments, but of course that's not what the author of the letter had in mind. Word your question carefully!

Your first paragraph is both the headline and the lead for the message that follows. Make your opening set the right tone with direct, positive phrases that establish a favorable impression with your reader.

> As soon as your letter arrived, we phoned your order to our St. Louis office.
>
> Your appointment as General Manager is good news indeed.
>
> You are right in assuming we want to hear from our customers.

Avoid openings that restate the obvious,

> I have received your letter of October 16...

have a negative tone,

> We cannot understand your failure to comply...

or use cliches,

> At Fletcher's, the customer is always right. So, better late than never, ...

People usually enjoy a tasteful anecdote or humorous quotation.

> Mark Twain had some good advice for investors when he said, "Put all your eggs in one basket—*and watch that basket!* At Prudential Guaranty, we're watching that basket for you.

Humor can backfire, however. Use it only with sensitivity to possible offense.

Do things first, and second things not at all.
—Peter Drucker

✎ Make your letter the right length.

A letter should be just long enough to do the job. Say what you have to say—politely, clearly, and briefly. You show the greatest consideration for readers when you take only enough of their time to convey what is important.

A book editor for the *Los Angeles Times* sent me the ultimate in brief letters. I had requested that my company, Periwinkle Press, be included in the *Times* file of publishers' addresses. This man believed that every letter deserved an answer, and his response consisted of one word: "Done."

In some cases, your response can be penned at the bottom or along the margins of a letter you received. For example, if someone writes asking a favor, you could indicate that you have complied by writing "I enclose the list of frequently misspelled words that you asked for" at the bottom of her letter. Or perhaps you receive an unsolicited letter promoting a product you're interested in; you could jot your response in the margin of a copy of the letter: "Please send me the specs for this widget."

Of course, most letters call for more than such casual brevity. But when you've used simple words and uncomplicated ways of expressing yourself, you have probably also been brief. That's a great virtue in today's busy world, as long as you haven't sacrificed clarity. Recipients of your letters will appreciate your having taken the time to avoid wasting theirs.

I have made this letter longer than usual because I lack the time to make it shorter.
—Blaise Pascal

⬧ Leave a good impression with your closing paragraph._____

The primary function of your final paragraph is to bring your letter to a courteous, businesslike close. Where suitable, you want to be persuasive. A summary of your letter is appropriate only if the letter is long. When action is called for, indicate what you want the reader to do or what you will do. Use positive words: "when" not "if."

Poor: Call me if you want more information.

Better: I will gladly provide more detailed information—just give me a call.

Poor: I will try to call you next week to see if we can find a convenient time to get together.

Better: I will call you next week to see when we can get together.

The amount of pressure you apply in your final paragraph depends on the nature of the letter. A goodwill letter that is primarily designed to keep in touch might end with a low-key closing:

"Let us hear from you when we can be of help."

You apply a little more pressure if you ask a question:

"May we send our sales representative, Jack Hammer, to demonstrate our new desktop model?"

Strongly urging a specific action is the high-pressure end of the spectrum. The reader should understand why it is advantageous to comply. The following examples suggest a few such cases:

Use the enclosed information sheet to order your copies today. The books will be on their way to you promptly.

Just fill out and mail the enclosed questionnaire. By return mail, we will send you a free 16-page booklet that's full of good advice on stretching your food budget.

Please send your check to cover the overdue balance promptly. I'm sure you don't want such a small amount to jeopardize your credit rating.

A weak ending can diminish the effectiveness of an otherwise well-written letter. Avoid the following:

Participial phrases

Thanking you in advance

Hoping for a favorable reply

An apologetic attitude

I'm sorry I haven't been of more help

Cliches

> At this point in time
>
> In the final analysis
>
> Last but not least

Make your closing sentences polite and to the point, and your reader will carry away a favorable impression.

FINAL STEPS

✆ Revising. _____

Revising turns the raw material of your letter into a polished product. When you have completed a letter, pause and "change hats" from author to reader. Review what you have written, asking yourself such questions as:

> Have I made my point(s)?
>
> Do the sentences and ideas flow smoothly?
>
> Have I avoided stilted language?
>
> Is the emphasis where I want it to be?
>
> Have I used the fewest possible words?

Allow enough time so that important letters can be put aside for a while. A letter going to thousands of potential customers or to one potential employer should be given a "cooling off" period—overnight or longer, if possible. You want to see the letter as if for the first time when you re-read it.

If you can, have someone else go over your draft as well. Ask for feedback on what they think your main ideas are and whether they would be convinced by your presentation if they were the recipients.

As you develop good habits, letter writing becomes easier. Letters that are short and straightforward will need little revision. In time, you will be able to edit in your head before you commit words to screen or paper. Still, you will always want to revise printouts of long or important letters; your words can invariably be tightened up and made more readable.

If you dictate your letters, revising is especially important. Spoken words often lose something in the process of being transcribed. The emphasis your voice gave to certain words may not appear, and the nuance you intended may be lost. Or you may have failed to notice that three sentences start with *however* until you saw the words on paper.

Revising to correct such faults is an essential part of the writing process. Malcolm Forbes, the late editor of *Forbes* magazine, demonstrated the process by striking out unneeded words in the following passage:

> Somebody ~~has~~ said that words are a lot like inflated money—the more ~~of them that~~ you use, the less each one ~~of them~~ is worth. ~~Right on.~~ Go through your entire letter ~~just~~ as many times as it takes. ~~Search out and~~ Annihilate all unnecessary words, ~~and~~ sentences—even ~~entire~~ paragraphs.

❧ Proofreading.

The last step before you send out a letter is to proofread it. Unfortunately, Murphy's Law of Proofreading is that you are most likely to miss errors in precisely those places where readers are most likely to notice them—namely, in the first lines of a paragraph, a page, a section, and in headings. Thus you should take extra care at every beginning. Here are some proofing techniques I have found helpful:

Read the letter aloud. Awkward phrases and grammatical glitches are more evident when you *hear* them.

Read it backwards, from bottom to top. This way, your eye doesn't slide past doubled words, since you aren't reading for meaning.

Use a dictionary or spell checker. Correct spelling is the most telling indication of a careful, educated writer. One wrong letter or a simple transposition turns *gather* into *father*, *marital* into *martial*. You can end up with embarrassments like the following:

> Look for prescription drugs on which the patients have expired.

Clearly, the correct word is *patents*, not *patients*. Be aware of the spell checker's limitations. It will catch most misspellings and doubled words that you may not have noticed, but it won't catch a mixup of homonyms like *there* and *their*.

When you've found one error, look for others nearby. Mistakes often come in clusters. Ironically, this may be the result of revising. When you edit, you may fail to notice the ripple effect caused by one change and leave behind stray words or phrases.

Look for double trouble. Is every opening parenthesis followed by a closing parenthesis? Do quotation marks come in pairs?

There's no safety in numbers. Proof numbers especially carefully. Errors there can be catastrophic.

Use a ruler or straightedge. This procedure keeps your eyes focused on the line you're reading, thus reducing the chance you will skip over something.

Check carefully where lines and pages break. Have any words been doubled or omitted?

Today's word processors make revising easy. You can add or delete words, rearrange sentences, insert paragraphs, and print a fresh copy in minutes. You can compare different versions of the same letter, side by side on the screen or printed out. You have the luxury of revising until your words are just right—until the sales letter is the most persuasive, the proposal most convincing, the job application most effective. Do it!

First impressions count. See page 48.

3 The Look of the Letter

Letter Placement and Design. . . . 48

Punctuating the Parts of a Business Letter. 49

Business Letter Format. 50

The Simplified Letter
The Block Letter
The Modified Block Letter
The Modified Semiblock Letter
The Official Letter
The Memorandum
The Fax Transmittal Form

The Elements of a Business Letter. 59

Envelopes 77

3 The Look of the Letter

First impressions can determine how your message will be received and whether your letter is read or tossed out. The first impression a letter makes is visual: Is it neat and well placed on the page? Does it please the eye?

Busy people look for ways to cut through the sea of paper confronting them. A well-formatted letter makes it easy for them to identify the main points quickly.

Of course, no amount of visual appeal can make up for a poorly written letter; ultimately, it has to stand on the strength of its content. But why handicap a well-written letter by putting it in an inferior package? If you observe a few simple principles, you can create a pleasing format that helps the reader concentrate on the substance of your letter.

LETTER PLACEMENT AND DESIGN

Think of a letter as a picture, with the margins serving as its frame. Set the left and right margins according to the length of the letter: 1″ for long letters (300+ words, 2 or more pages), $1^1/_2$″ for average letters (100–300 words), and 2″ for short letters (fewer than 100 words).

The stationery you use also influences placement of the letter. Letterheads vary widely, from flashy to sedate, from inconspicuous to space-consuming. Aim for balance between the letterhead and the letter itself. For example, if the company logo fills the upper left corner, you could put the date flush with the right margin. If the company name and address is centered on the page, center the dateline under it. Balance a list of names printed along the left margin of the letterhead by placing the date, complimentary close, and signature on the right-hand side of the page.

If you are typing on plain paper instead of letterhead, place the return address and dateline according to the letter format you have chosen (see pp. 50-57). A centered return address is usually placed a little higher on the page (1″ to $1^1/_2$″ below the top edge) than a return address that is flush left or on the right side ($1^1/_2$″ to 2″ below the top). The number of lines in the return address and the length of the letter determine where the return address is placed within these ranges. Type the date on the line directly below the return address. If the return address is centered, center the date as well.

Avoid the extremes. A short letter placed high on the page looks as if the writer ran out of things to say, while a long letter in which the signature block is squeezed onto the bottom of the page gives the impression of poor planning.

To make a short letter fill the page, increase the space between the various elements of the letter: between date and inside address, between inside address and salutation, between complimentary close and signature block, and between signature block and any notations. To make a long letter less crowded, edit the text to make it shorter or start an additional page; carry over at least three lines of text to the continuation sheet.

Use single-space for the lines within paragraphs and double-space between paragraphs. Set the margins of continuation pages to match the first page. Include the date, name of addressee, and page number at the top of any continuation pages. (See "Letters of More Than One Page," p. 69.)

Word processors enable you to create an attractive letterhead. Such word-processor-generated letterheads are useful for routine business matters or for informal correspondence, but printed letterhead remains the norm for most business correspondence.

LETTER PLACEMENT

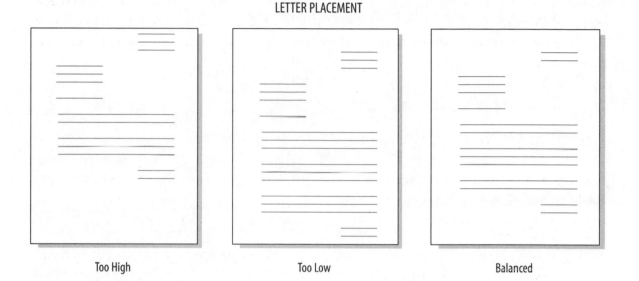

Too High   Too Low   Balanced

Punctuating the Parts of a Business Letter

The questions about punctuation that concern today's letter writer are pragmatic: Do I need punctuation at the end of each address line? What kind of punctuation should I use with the salutation? Does the punctuation in my letters look conventional?

The following rules are both traditional and easy to observe. (If you need help with punctuation within the text of the letter, refer to *Write Right!* or one of the other handbooks listed in "Resources for the Letter Writer," p. 182.)

(1) Use no punctuation after the date.

January 2, 2005

(2) Use no punctuation at the *end* of each line of the inside address.

11500 Century Plaza, 11th Floor

except:

(3) Use a period following an abbreviation.

Widgetron, Inc.

(4) Use a colon with the salutation in a business letter.

Dear Ms. Stake:

(5) Use a comma with the salutation in a personal letter.

Dear Hank,

(6) Use a comma with the complimentary close.

Yours truly,

(7) Use no punctuation after the writer's name.

Miss Pearl E. Gates

BUSINESS LETTER FORMAT

Today, businesspeople doing their own keyboarding aren't interested in the differences between letter styles with fancy names (Block, Modified Block, Modified Semiblock, and so on). What they want is a neat, efficient letter style that they don't have to think about. Fortunately, word processors make this easy.

With the attributes available at the click of a mouse (such as italics and boldface), and with a wide variety of fonts and type sizes to choose from, you can design letters that both appeal to the eye and help convey your message. But don't overdo in using all the bells and whistles at your disposal or your letter will become visually distracting.

If you establish your most frequently used format as the default setting or as a template for your letters, choices regarding spacing and placement of the various elements will be automatic. Many word processors come with several letter formats already established; all you have to do is call them up and begin typing. Placement and spacing of the various elements of the letter, including spacing between paragraphs, is done for you.

The main variable in letter formats is placement of the date and the complimentary close. Some people like the ease of the Block style, because all lines begin flush with the left margin. Others prefer the more balanced appearance of Modified Block and Semiblock, in which the date and complimentary close begin near the centerline of the page.

The Simplified Letter solves the problem of devising a nonsexist salutation by eliminating it. With no salutation, you don't have to worry about offending someone with *Dear Sirs* or addressing a woman as *Mr.* However, if you know the recipient's name and gender, I recommend that you choose one of the block style formats; letters with a salutation and complimentary close are less abrupt and more friendly than the Simplified Letter.

The Official format is used for personal letters in business (for example, a thank-you note to a professional colleague). Memos are widely used for informal business correspondence; they have the advantage of quickly formatting a note while eliminating the salutation problem.

The following pages first illustrate the most commonly used format styles and then discuss the various parts of the letter.

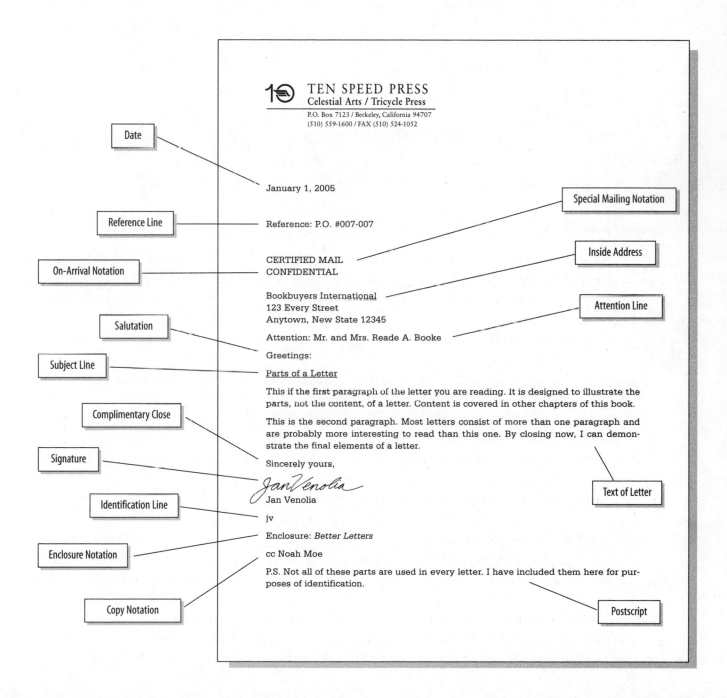

The Simplified Letter

- Use no salutation.
- Begin all lines flush with the left margin.
- Place the date six lines below the letterhead.
- Place the inside address three or four lines below the dateline. Abbreviate the state, using the two capital letters designated by the Postal Service.
- Type the subject in caps, three lines below the inside address and above the body of the letter; do not use the words "Subject" or "Re."
- Do not use a complimentary close.
- Type the writer's name and title, in caps, four or five lines below the body of the letter.

✓ Simplified Letter Format
✓ Sales Letter

Dee Klein & Associates
INVESTMENT COUNSELING
502 Park Avenue / New York, New York 10006 / Telephone (212) 233-5577 / Fax (212) 255-5500

6 lines —

January 30, 2005

3-4 lines —

Justin Case, Esquire
190 Avenue of the Planets, Suite 1234
Brentwood, CA 90071

3 lines —

ARE YOUR EARNINGS WORKING FOR YOU?

3 lines —

Over the years, we have observed that lawyers are good at making money but poor at investing it. They provide excellent legal advice for their clients, and then fail to obtain the expert advice they themselves need in financial matters.

Klein & Associates specializes in serving the legal community. We understand that your time is heavily committed, since a good legal practice demands much of the partners. What you need is a financial advisor who produces results--consistently.

I enclose a list of our clients in your area. We have been able to develop this prestigious clientele by making their capital grow. Furthermore, Klein counselors know how to keep them beyond the reach of the IRS on the one hand, and the Justice Department on the other.

Let us add your name to our list. If we help you invest your earnings, you may find your name appearing on another list as well--the Forbes 400!

4-5 lines —

ASA DIAMOND
Vice-President

2 lines —

Enclosure

The Block Letter

- Begin all lines flush with the left margin.
- Do not indent paragraphs.
- Place the dateline two to six lines below the letterhead.
- Place the inside address two to six lines below the dateline.
- Place the salutation two to four lines below the inside address.
- If a subject line is used, capitalize it and place it two lines below the salutation.
- Begin typing the text two lines below the salutation or subject line.
- Place the complimentary close two lines below text.
- Place the signature block four lines below the complimentary close.
- Put notations such as Distribution or Enclosure two lines below the signature block; if identification initials are used, include only those of the typist.

✓ Block Letter Format
✓ Response to Complaint

The Downes Roofing Company

712 Broadway / Central City, South Dakota 57402 / Telephone (123) 456-7800 / Fax (123) 456-7888

2-6 lines

July 15, 2005

2-6 lines

Mr. and Mrs. R. T. Choke
22 North Parkway
Central City, South Dakota 57401

2-4 lines

2 lines

Dear Mr. and Mrs. Choke:

Our attorney and insurance agent are sorting out the liabilities stemming from our agreement to re-roof your house. As you know, the problem started when my secretary couldn't read your handwriting and the contract was drawn up with the wrong address. When you went out of town in order to avoid the dirt and noise of re-roofing, we had the ingredients of a tragedy.

We might still have discovered the error in time if your neighbors had not also been out of town when my crew arrived at 23 North Parkway instead of 22 North Parkway. As it is, however, you still have a leaky roof, we haven't been paid for the roof we installed at 23 North Parkway, and your neighbors are upset at having their two-year-old tile roof replaced with composition shingles.

As soon as I hear from my advisors, I will let you know their suggestions for resolving this complicated problem.

2 lines

Very truly yours,

4 lines

Upson Downes
President

2 lines

/jgv

The Modified Block Letter

- Place the date two to six lines below the letterhead, either flush with the right margin or about five spaces to the right of center.
- Begin the inside address flush with the left margin, two to six lines below the date-line.
- Type the salutation flush with the left margin, two to four lines below the inside address.
- Align the complimentary close and signature block with the date; leave two lines between the text of the letter and the close, and four or five lines between the close and the writer's typed name.

✓ Modified Block Letter Format
✓ Publicity Release

POWER GRAPHICS, INC.

7512 Peachblossom Street, Suite 425 • Atlanta, Georgia 36541
(987) 654-3212 / FAX (987) 654-8769

2-6 lines

April 30, 2005

2-6 lines

KYRU
Media Tower
One Fall Street
Los Angeles, CA 90000

2 lines

Attention Programming Department

2-4 lines

Greetings:

2 lines

Mark your calendars: May 15. That's when Power Graphics opens its Los Angeles office with a major media event--one that combines Will Power's flair for publicity with his interest in redistributing wealth.

At noon on May 15, Mr. Power and his brothers A.C. and D.C. will step onto the roof of the Downtown Biltless Hotel. An assistant will carry four large boxes of $10 bills. The Power brothers will proceed to drop the bills, one at a time, to the streets below. The total to be "thrown to the winds" in this way is a closely guarded secret, but as you know, Mr. Power doesn't believe in halfway measures.

Think of the photo opportunities, the stories, the camera angles as your crews pan the chaos in the streets below the hotel. It will be an epic of Cecil D. Schlemiel proportions! Power Graphics will work closely with the media to assure saturation coverage. However, we can schedule an exclusive interview with KYRU's Dan Somewhat, if you call to make arrangements immediately.

2 lines

Sincerely yours,

4-5 lines

Page Turner
Page Turner
Publicity Department

The Modified Semiblock Letter

- Place the date two to six lines below the letterhead, either flush with the right margin or about five spaces to the right of center.
- Type the salutation two to four lines below the dateline.
- If a subject line is used, type it in caps, centered, two lines below the salutation.
- Indent the first line of each paragraph five or ten spaces.
- Align the complimentary close and signature block with the date, beginning two lines below the text and allowing four or five lines for the signature.
- If a postscript is used, place it two to four lines below the last notation.

✓ Modified Semiblock Letter Format
✓ Request for Action with Subject Line

2-6 lines

2-6 lines

2-4 lines

2 lines

2 lines

2 lines

4-5 lines

2 lines

DREW PROCESS, ESQUIRE
190 Avenue of the Stars, Suite 1234, Los Angeles, California 90073
Telephone (213) 321-6789, Fax (213) 321-9908

May 17, 2005

Mr. Will Power, President
Power Graphics, Inc.
7512 Peachblossom Street, Suite 425
Atlanta, GA 36543

Dear Mr. Power:

SUBJECT: MAY 15 MEDIA EVENT

The City of Los Angeles has asked me to notify you of their position concerning your media event of May 15, 2005. You may have thought that only good could flow from dropping $10 bills from a hotel rooftop; the City has a different view.

The publicity surrounding the event assured a large crowd. In fact, people started camping along the sidewalks as early as May 13. It took crowd control personnel and clean-up crews from all parts of the city working double shifts to maintain some degree of order.

Few $10 bills were found in the litter left by the crowds, but the litter itself left the City with a large bill: $25,000 for clean-up alone. When combined with other costs the City incurred, the total exceeds $75,000.

Littering is a misdemeanor, and inciting to riot is a felony. However, the mayor and council will not press those charges if Power Graphics will pay $75,000 to cover the City's costs. I trust you can see the reasonableness of their proposal. Please send your check, payable to the City of Los Angeles, by May 30.

Very truly yours,

Drew Process

Drew Process

Copies to: Mayor Nan O. Second
Members of the City Council

The Official Letter

- Place the date flush with the right margin, two to six lines below the letterhead.

- Allow two to twelve lines between the date and the salutation, and two lines below the salutation before beginning the text of the letter.

- Place the complimentary close two lines below the text, about five spaces to the right of center.

- Omit the typed signature block.

- Begin the inside address two to five lines below the signature.

- Place any optional identification line and enclosure notations two lines below the address.

- Use this format for personal letters written by an executive on personalized company letterhead.

✓ Official Letter Format
✓ Business Thank-You Letter

CITY OF ORANGE GROVE

500 MAIN STREET • ORANGE GROVE, FLORIDA 33030

Office of the City Manager *Phone (302) 555-3333 • Fax (302) 555-3211*

2-6 lines

October 12, 2005

2-12 lines

2 lines

Dear Jack:

You gave our Aquarium Development Project just the boost it needed. The Ways & Means Committee reports that our fund-raising drive is over the top, thanks to your Traveling Troop of Trained Porpoises. I truly appreciated your letting me draw on our old school ties when you agreed to come to Orange Grove.

Your show created quite a stir in town. Teaching the porpoises to twist themselves into the shape of dollar signs was inspired! The audience had no chance to forget why they were there.

The TV crews really zeroed in on the sinking ship sequence. I'm sure the Chamber of Commerce members who saw it didn't miss the significance of seeing the S.S. City of Orange Grove go under because it didn't beef up its tourist industry.

Hazel and I look forward to having you with us in May for the ground-breaking ceremonies. Give our regards to Stephanie, and be sure to bring her with you for the big event next spring.

2 lines

Cordially,

4 lines

2-5 lines

Mr. Jack Cass
Miami Porpoise Headquarters
678 Bricknell Road
Miami, Florida 33333

The Memorandum

About two inches from the top of the page, place the four standard Memo headings: To, From, Date, and Subject. (These headings are already established in a word processor's Memo format; they are also frequently printed as company stationery.)

- Double-space the headings.

- Use no salutation or complimentary close.

- The writer's initials are optional.

✓ Memorandum Format

TO: Personnel Staff

FROM: Al E. Katz

DATE: September 15, 2005

SUBJECT: Screening Procedures

Effective immediately, all applicants for positions with Hydrodynamics are to be given Personality Adjustment Series J Tests. These will replace the Series H Test that was used previously.

The new series is both easier to administer and to evaluate. I trust you will find it helps your task of selecting qualified candidates for employment.

AEK

The Fax Transmittal Form

If you don't already have a printed fax transmittal page, create one. Include the following information:

- Sender's name, address, phone and fax numbers
- Date
- Recipient's name, address, phone and fax numbers
- Total number of pages being faxed, including the cover letter

Number the pages you are sending to make it easier for the recipient to determine that they have all arrived. Don't use colored paper or correction fluid.

✓ Fax Transmittal Form

TEN SPEED PRESS

Celestial Arts / Tricycle Press
P.O. Box 7123, Berkeley, California 94707
Phone (510) 559-1600 / Fax (510) 524-1052

Company: _____ Attn: _____

FAX #: _____ From: _____

# of pgs (including this page): _____ Date: _____

Please let us know if all pages are NOT received

Message: _____

_____

_____

_____

_____

The Elements of a Business Letter

✎ Date.

Place the date on a single line two to six lines below the letterhead, depending on the length of the letter. Letter format determines whether the date is flush with the right or left margin, a few spaces to the right of center, or centered under the letterhead address. Do not allow the dateline to run into the margin.

Do not abbreviate or use figures for the month; for example, do not type *Dec. 25* or *12/25/05*. Do not use ordinals *(1st, 14th,* etc.). The standard order of month and day *(December 25, 2005)* may be reversed and the comma omitted *(25 December 2005)* when writing to the U.S. Government, military personnel, or correspondents in foreign countries.

STANDARD DATELINE POSITIONS

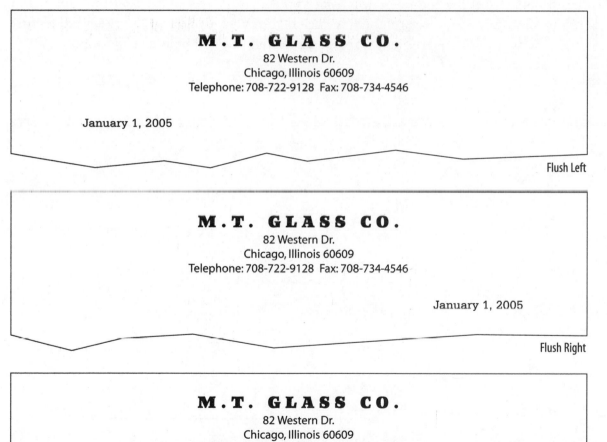

M.T. GLASS CO.
82 Western Dr.
Chicago, Illinois 60609
Telephone: 708-722-9128 Fax: 708-734-4546

January 1, 2005

Right of Center

⬧ **Reference line.**

If an incoming letter has a numerical reference, type the number cited one to four lines below the dateline in your response. The reference line is flush with the left margin in the Block Letter, but may be blocked left or right in other formats. If your company also has a policy of using file references, place your own reference number one line below the incoming reference or on the line included in your company letterhead. Reference lines are typical of government correspondence and can be helpful when writing about an order.

TANYA HYDE LEATHER CO.
410 Cambridge Ave.
Buffalo, New York 14225
(716) 123-4567
Fax:(716) 987-6543

October 22, 2005

Reference: P.O. #593-82E
Our File Ref.: Invoice #6829

Reference Line

⬧ **Special mailing notations.**

Some companies want any unusual mailing features noted: EXPRESS MAIL, CERTIFIED MAIL, FED-EX, etc. Others prefer that mailing notations appear only on copies of the letter. Still others omit this type of notation altogether. If a mailing notation is used, place it flush with the left margin, about four lines below the dateline and two lines above the inside address in all letter formats.

M.T. GLASS CO.
82 Western Dr.
Chicago, Illinois 60609
Telephone: 708-722-9128 Fax: 708-734-4546

March 1, 2005

EXPRESS MAIL

Mr. Steve Adohr
CMP Corporation
87 North Blvd.
Johnson, TX 75623

Special Mailing Notation

On-arrival notations.

If a business letter is personal, write the word *Personal* or *Confidential*, underlined, at the top of the letter. Place it flush with the left margin, about four lines above the inside address. The word must also appear on the envelope, about nine lines below the top edge. If you use both special mailing and on-arrival notations, place the on-arrival notation immediately below the special mailing notation.

Personal indicates that a letter is to be opened and read only by its addressee; *Confidential* indicates that a letter may be opened and read by any person so authorized. Reserve the use of this notation for matters that are indeed personal, rather than as a device to catch someone's attention.

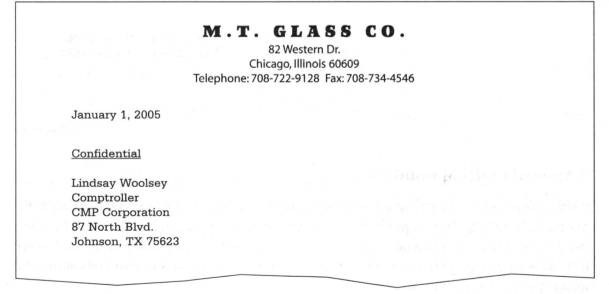

M.T. GLASS CO.
82 Western Dr.
Chicago, Illinois 60609
Telephone: 708-722-9128 Fax: 708-734-4546

January 1, 2005

Confidential

Lindsay Woolsey
Comptroller
CMP Corporation
87 North Blvd.
Johnson, TX 75623

On-Arrival Notation

✑ Inside address.

In all but the Official style, place the address of the recipient (the inside address) three to eight lines below the dateline. The inside address is always flush with the left margin and single-spaced.

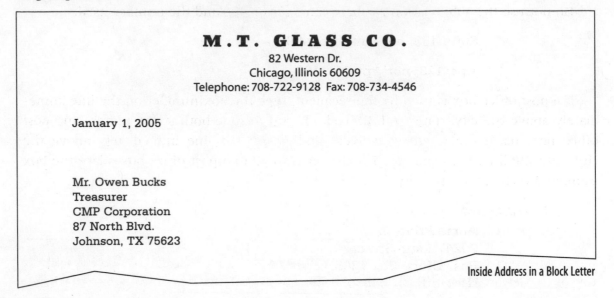

M.T. GLASS CO.
82 Western Dr.
Chicago, Illinois 60609
Telephone: 708-722-9128 Fax: 708-734-4546

January 1, 2005

Mr. Owen Bucks
Treasurer
CMP Corporation
87 North Blvd.
Johnson, TX 75623

Inside Address in a Block Letter

If a line of the address would extend beyond the middle of the page, break it into two lines at a convenient spot, indenting the carryover line two spaces.

> Ms. Adah Mellon
> Tri-State Nickel Plate Quality Assurance
>   and Underwriters Association
> 1234 Broad Street
> Andover, NY 10022

When addressing a specific individual at a company, place the individual's name on the first line, and the company name on the second. Use the official company name, including abbreviations, capitalization, ampersands (&), and other stylistic conventions employed by the company you are addressing.

> Mr. Al Dentay
> Simple Simon Pie & Tart Co., Ltd.

When the letter is addressed to a specific department within a company rather than to an individual, type the company name on the first line and the department on the second.

> The June Company Department Stores
> Credit Department
> One Broad Street
> Jackson, MS 39558

Place suite, room, or apartment numbers *after* and on the same line as the street address, separated by a comma.

> 1234 Spring Street, Suite 1157
> Los Angeles, CA 90017

Do not use the abbreviation *No.* between *Suite* or *Apt.* and the number itself.

> Suite 456, *not* Suite No. 456
>
> Apt. 123, *not* Apt. No. 123

If a post office box is used by the recipient, type the box number on the line immediately above the city, state, and ZIP code. If you include both street address and post office box, place the intended delivery address on the line immediately above the city/state/ZIP line. For example, if the letter is to go to a post office box, place the box number directly above the city line.

> *To be delivered to post office:*
> Acme Printers
> 20247 Main Street
> Post Office Box 1305
> Newton, OR 96830

If the letter is to be delivered to the street address, place that line directly above the city line.

> *To be delivered to street address:*
> Acme Printers
> Post Office Box 1305
> 20247 Main Street
> Newton, OR 96837

Be sure the ZIP code matches whichever address is above the city line.

Spell out compass directions that *precede* the street name; abbreviate those *following* it.

> 1234 West Orange Street   567 Lemon Street SW

The word *One* is written out in a street address; all other numbers appear as figures.

> One Market Street   359 James Street

Numbered streets are written as words for twelve and below, and usually as figures above twelve. However, some prefer the more formal appearance of words for numbered streets. When figures are used, insert a spaced hyphen between the building number and the street number.

> 300 Seventh Avenue
>
> 750 - 22nd Street   *or*   750 Twenty-second Street

⌂ Titles.

A courtesy title (*Mr., Dr., Ms.*) precedes the name of the addressee, and, where applicable, a professional title follows the addressee's surname (last name).

Dr. Jerry Atrick, Chief of Staff

Mr. Landon Bridges, C.P.A.

Place long professional titles on the second line of the address.

Ms. Iona Howes
Vice President and General Manager

Omit the courtesy title if the name is followed by *Esq.* or by an abbreviation for a degree.

N. R. Childe, M.D.

Terry A. Weil, Esq.

When addressing more than one individual, place the names on separate lines in alphabetical order, not "Ladies First" order.

Mr. Harold Angell
Ms. Sarah Fimm
M.T. Glass Company
82 Western Drive
Chicago, IL 60609

Dear Mr. Angell and Ms. Fimm:

Messrs., which is the abbreviation of *Messieurs* (the plural form of *Mr.*), may be used when addressing more than one male.

Mr. Grant Ryder
Mr. Jay Walker
Crimea River Development
73$^1/_2$ Odessa Circle
Hyattsville, MD 20781

Dear Messrs. Ryder and Walker:

Address more than one female as *Mesdames, Mmes.,* or *Mses.*

Ms. Marion Spring
Ms. Augusta Winde
Entre News Publishing
P.O. Box 7321
Minneapolis, MN 55410

Dear Mses. Spring and Winde:

When addressing a couple where one or both are titled, you have additional choices. When both have a title:

Drs. Dodie and Earl E. Byrd

or Dr. Dodie Byrd and Dr. Earl E. Byrd

or Drs. Earl E. and Dodie Byrd

Rev. Lettice Prey and Dr. Paul Bearer

or Dr. Paul Bearer and Rev. Lettice Prey

When only one has a title:

in business correspondence:

Dr. Fan C. Dresser and Mr. Nat T. Dresser

The Honorable Clem N. See and Ms. Eve Adam

Col. Luce Sum and Mrs. Win Sum

in social correspondence:

Dr. and Mrs. Hale N. Hardy

or Dr. Hale N. Hardy and Mrs. Laurel Ann Hardy

or Dr. and Mrs. Hale and Laurel Ann Hardy

Ms. Ginger Ailes and Mr. Foster Holmes

or Ms. Ginger Ailes

Mr. Foster Holmes

Whenever it is known, use the form preferred by the individual(s) you are addressing. People are usually sensitive about their name and will notice if you get it right—or wrong.

In the past, if the gender of an individual was unknown, a masculine title was used. As one who dislikes receiving letters addressed to *Mr.* Jan Venolia, I recommend that you omit any courtesy title when you don't know the gender of the recipient. If a salutation is needed, use the addressee's full name: Dear Jan Venolia.

✆ Attention line.

Use an attention line when your letter is addressed to a company or organization in general but you wish to bring it to the attention of a specific individual. Place the attention line flush with the left margin, two lines below the last line of the inside address. Do not abbreviate the word *Attention*; a colon following the word is optional.

Attention: Ms. Olive Pitts

or Attention Ms. Olive Pitts

Since the letter is addressed primarily to the company, use a group salutation: *Greetings* or *Ladies and Gentlemen*.

M.T. GLASS CO.
82 Western Dr.
Chicago, Illinois 60609
Telephone: 708-722-9128 Fax: 708-734-4546

March 1, 2005

CMP Corporation
Advertising Department
87 North Blvd.
Johnson, TX 75623

Attention: Mr. Jon Quill

Greetings:

Attention Line in a Block Letter

◧ Salutation.

The salutation is omitted in the Simplified Letter; in all other letter styles it is flush left, two lines below the last line of the inside address or the attention line, if used. The salutation is followed by a colon in business correspondence and by a comma in personal letters.

The standard *Dear Mrs. Sippi* or *Dear John* is appropriate for most situations, including the very formal. *My dear Mrs. Sippi* would only be used when addressing dignitaries (see Appendix C, "Forms of Address," p. 161).

When you do not know who the addressee is (for example, in some letters of recommendation), you have a number of alternatives to choose from. You can avoid the outdated flavor of *To Whom It May Concern* and the awkwardness of *Dear Sir or Madam* by using the Simplified Letter or the Memo format, which eliminate the salutation. You can also use generic categories.

Dear Friend	Dear Customer	Dear Supporter
Dear Homeowner	Dear Board Member	Dear Parents

For a more complete discussion of this and other aspects of sexist terms in letters, see Chapter 4, "Dear Sir or Madam."

✍ Subject line.

The subject line identifies the content of the letter in a few well-chosen words. It is part of the body of the letter and thus is placed two spaces below the salutation, either centered or flush left. In the Simplified Letter, which has no salutation, the subject line is placed flush left, three lines below the last line of the inside address.

M.T. GLASS CO.
82 Western Dr.
Chicago, Illinois 60609
Telephone: 708-722-9128 Fax: 708-734-4546

January 1, 2005

Furst & Foremost Management Consultants
1123 Hyde St.
Jacksonville, FL 37890

SIMPLIFIED LETTER FORMAT

We would like to introduce the Simplified Letter to Furst & Foremost. The advantages of this new letter format are....

Subject Line in a Simplified Letter

M.T. GLASS CO.
82 Western Dr.
Chicago, Illinois 60609
Telephone: 708-722-9128 Fax: 708-734-4546

January 1, 2005

Furst & Foremost Management Consultants
1123 Hyde St.
Jacksonville, FL 37890

Ladies and Gentlemen:

NEW PROFIT-SHARING POLICY

We would like to acquaint the employees of Furst & Foremost with our new policy, which we feel will benefit everyone....

Subject Line in a Block Letter

The word *Subject* is optional, as is the colon following it. You may use all caps and no underlining or capitalize the first letter in each important word and underline the entire subject line.

SUBJECT: THE ANNUAL SHAREHOLDERS' MEETING

or

The Annual Shareholders' Meeting

Text.

Begin the text of your message three lines below the subject line in the Simplified Letter and two lines below the salutation or subject line in all other letter styles. Use single-space for most letters, with double-space between paragraphs. If a letter is very short, you may use space-and-a-half or double-space. Indent paragraphs five or ten spaces when using the Semiblock and Official styles, or when the letter is double-spaced.

Indent or center numbered material in the body of a letter. Single-space within each item, and double-space between items. Set off long quoted material from the rest of the letter by indenting it.

In general, avoid abbreviating words in the text of a letter; exceptions are social or professional titles (*Dr., Mrs.,* etc.) or words that are usually abbreviated, such as company names (*Beecham Intl., Ltd.*). Abbreviating other words gives the impression that you are too rushed or uninterested to be more careful. I once received a letter from a department store addressing me as "Dear Cust." The space and time saved by not typing the remaining four letters were a poor bargain for the store.

Dividing Words. Observe the following rules for hyphenating words at the right-hand margin.

- Avoid hyphenating as much as possible.

- Do not divide a word at the end of the first line of a letter.

- Do not divide the last word of a letter or paragraph.

- Hyphenate according to dictionary syllabication.

- Never separate one letter from the rest of the word, either at the beginning or end of a line.

- Do not carry the final two letters over to the next line.

Wrong:	Right:
time-	timely
ly	

- Never hyphenate a one-syllable word.

- Avoid dividing compound words that are already hyphenated.

Wrong:	Right:
fif- ty-five	fifty- five
end-of-sea- son	end-of- season

Do not divide a word in a person's name or separate a name from the courtesy or professional title.

Wrong:	Right:
Lacey Valen- tine	Lacey Valentine
Dr. Sonny Schein	Dr. Sonny Schein

If possible, do not separate the parts of a name, date, or address. When necessary, separate as follows.

Ms. Robin D. Craydell	Art N. Kraft	Sgt. Aaron Tyres
July 1, 1905	395 Broad Street	Middletown, OH 44015

Break a numbered list before, not after, the number or letter.

Wrong:

(1) _____, (2) _____, (3)

_____.

Right:

(1) _____, (2) _____,

(3) _____.

Never separate a long number.

Wrong:	Right:
345,000, 000	345,000,000

Letters of More Than One Page. Use printed letterhead only for the first page of a letter. Type continuation pages on plain sheets that match the letterhead stationery or on printed second sheets. Carry over at least three lines of text to any continuation pages, and make the margins the same as on the first page.

Type the heading for second sheets six lines below the top of the page and include the addressee's name, the page number, and the date. Leave four or five lines between the heading and the text of the letter on continuation sheets.

In the Simplified and Block Letter, the heading items are flush left.

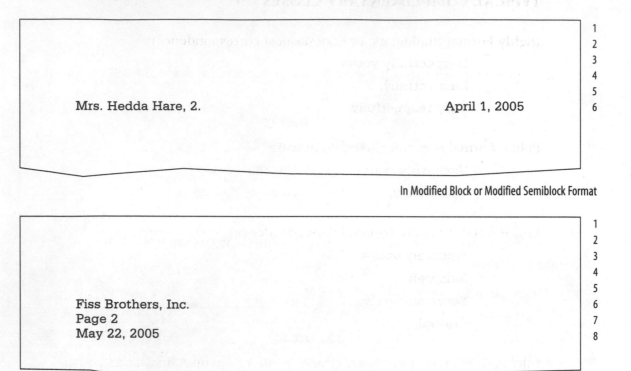

	1
	2
	3
	4
	5
Mrs. Hedda Hare, 2. April 1, 2005	6

In Modified Block or Modified Semiblock Format

	1
	2
	3
	4
	5
Fiss Brothers, Inc.	6
Page 2	7
May 22, 2005	8

In Simplified or Block Format

If the letter is addressed to two individuals, both names appear on the continuation pages.

	1
	2
	3
	4
	5
Mr. Clay Bowles May 14, 2005	6
Mr. Lee Ward Page 2	7

When you write to more than one individual at a firm

✆ Complimentary close.

The complimentary close is placed two lines below the text of the letter, either flush with the left margin (Block), aligned with the date (Modified Block), or a few spaces to the right of center (Modified Semiblock, Official). It should never extend beyond the right margin established by the body of the letter.

Capitalize only the first letter of the first word of a complimentary close; end it with a comma.

TYPICAL COMPLIMENTARY CLOSES

Highly Formal (diplomatic or ecclesiastical correspondence):

> **Respectfully yours,**
>
> **Respectfully,**
>
> **Very respectfully,**

Polite, Formal (general correspondence):

> **Very truly yours,**
>
> **Yours truly,**

Less Formal, Friendly (general correspondence):

> **Sincerely yours,**
>
> **Sincerely,**
>
> **Yours sincerely,**
>
> **Cordially,**

Informal, Friendly (when writer and recipient are on a first-name basis):

> **As ever,**
>
> **Best regards,**
>
> **Best wishes,**
>
> **Regards,**
>
> **Kindest personal regards,**
>
> **Yours,**

◊ **Signature.**_____

The signature block is aligned with, and four or five lines below, the complimentary close. It consists of the writer's name in the form preferred by the writer (e.g., G. V. Train, Gray V. Train) and the writer's title. If a title is used, it is placed on the same line as the name or one line below it.

> **Very truly yours,**
>
> *G. V. Train*
>
> **G. V. Train, President**

or   Sincerely yours,

Gray V. Train

Gray V. Train
Vice President and General Manager

Very truly yours,

Iona Howes

Iona Howes
Manager, Astronautics Department

gbb

Complimentary Close and Signature Block in the Block Letter

In the Simplified Letter, the writer's name is typed all in caps, flush with the left margin, four or five lines below the body of the letter.

Alan Wrench

ALAN WRENCH
CHIEF OPERATING OFFICER

gbb

Signature Block in the Simplified Letter

If letterhead stationery is used, do not include the company name in the signature block; if letterhead is not used, type the company name in caps two lines below the complimentary close, and the writer's name (only initial letters capitalized) four lines below the company name.

Very truly yours,

POTTS MANUFACTURING COMPANY

(signature)

Jack Potts, President

If the letter deals with personal matters, omit the writer's title. The department name, business title, and writer's name may be omitted if they appear in the letterhead.

If title and department do not appear on letterhead:	Charity Ball, Director Community Relations
If department appears on letterhead:	Charity Ball, Director
If title and department appear on letterhead:	Charity Ball

When a letter states a professional opinion or gives professional advice, some prefer to type the company name before the writer's name. In this case, type the company name in caps two lines below the complimentary close; type the word *By* and a line for the signature of the writer four spaces below the company name, and the writer's name and title directly below the line.

Very truly yours,

SEASIDE PROPERTIES, INC.

By _C. R. Holmes_

C. R. Holmes, Broker

When two people sign a letter, place the names on the same line, with the first name flush with the left margin.

Very truly yours,

(signature)   *(signature)*

Sue E. Generous   Don E. Brooke
Chair   Treasurer

Complimentary Close and Signature Block when Two People Sign a Letter

If there isn't room for both names on one line, place the second name four spaces below the first signature block.

Very truly yours,

Sue E. Generous

Sue E. Generous, Chair

Don E. Brooke

Don E. Brooke, Treasurer

Complimentary Close and Signature Block when Two People Sign a Letter

If you are signing a letter for the writer, place your initials just below and to the right of the signature.

Sincerely yours,

Sylvan Woods
          mb

Sylvan Woods, President

When you write a letter on behalf of your employer or supervisor (that is, you actually compose the letter), type your name above a descriptive title.

(1)   Very truly yours,

Maury Bund

Maury Bund
Assistant to Senator Stump

(2)   Sincerely yours,

Wanda Rownde

Wanda Rownde
Secretary to Ms. Nomer

> Sincerely yours,
>
> *Eaton Crowe*
>
> Eaton Crowe
> Assistant to Miss Ann Thrope

Complimentary Close and Signature Block in the Modified Block Letter

Identification line.

An identification line showing the initials of the typist is optional. Many organizations place identifying initials only on copies of the letter, for record-keeping purposes. The initials of the writer are typed in uppercase, and of the typist in lowercase. They are usually typed flush left, two lines below the signature block; they may follow a colon or slash.

TMS/lah	lh
TMS:lah	/lah
lah	:lh

Enclosure notation.

Enclosure notations serve both as a check to the recipient of the letter that everything was actually enclosed and as a reminder to the letter writer of what was sent. The unabbreviated word *Enclosure(s)* is typed flush left, two spaces below the identification line, if used. If more than one document is enclosed, list the number in parentheses or identify them, one per line.

> Sincerely yours,
>
> *Y.R. Cutter*
>
> Y.R. Cutter
> Program Manager
>
> gbb
>
> Enclosures (7)

Identification and Enclosure Notations in the Block Letter

Very truly yours,

Wright O'Way

Wright O'Way

Enclosures: 1. Check for $250.00
             2. Resale Tax Card
             3. Registration Form

Enclosure Notation in the Modified Block or Semiblock Letter

Copy notation.

If you wish the recipient to know of distribution of copies of the letter, type *Copy to* and the name of the individual(s) flush left, two lines below all other notations. The abbreviation *cc* (courtesy copy) may also be used. Courtesy copies are not usually signed.

Very truly yours,

Sue Flay

Sue Flay
Secretary

Copy to Mrs. Millie Second

Cordially,

R.T. Fiss

R.T. Fiss
Editor

/gbb

cc Ms. Sippi

Identification and Copy Notations in the Modified Block Letter

List multiple recipients of copies alphabetically.

    cc: Ms. Gates
         Mr. Holmes
         Mr. Woods

If you don't want the recipient to know of copy distribution, enter blind copy nota-tion (*bcc*) on copies of the letter only, either in the same page position or in the upper left-hand corner.

🖹 Postscript.

A postscript is typed flush left, two to four spaces below the last notation. The initials *P.S.* preceding the postscript are optional. Use postscripts sparingly. They should never sug-gest that you omitted information and had to tack it on at the end. But since they do catch the reader's eye, postscripts can be used effectively in a sales letter.

Mark Twain put the postscript to good use in the following letter to Andrew Carnegie:

Dear Sir and Friend:

You seem to be in prosperity. Could you lend an admirer $1.50 to buy a hymn book with? God will bless you. I feel it; I know it. So will I.

                    Yours,

                    Mark

P.S. Don't send the hymn book; send the money; I want to make the selection myself.

ENVELOPES

Postal Service automation, with its optical character readers (OCR) and barcode sorters, places certain requirements on the address that appears on an envelope. To take full advantage of this computerized system, you should adhere to the basic rules below. If you do extensive mailings, request copies of the pertinent publications from the Postal Service. (See "Resources for the Letter Writer," p. 182.)

The Postal Service recommends that *all* envelopes be addressed properly for machine readability. This means typing the entire address in capital letters, in addition to the spec-ifications described below. If you wish to avoid such a "mass mailing" look, you can opt instead for the more visually pleasing—and formal—appearance of upper- and lowercase letters with minimal abbreviations. Your letters will still be accepted and processed.

✎ Envelope size.

Letter envelopes should be no smaller than $3^1/_2''$ by $5''$ and no larger than $6^1/_8''$ by $11^1/_2''$. Envelopes smaller than the minimum are not mailable; larger envelopes can be mailed, but they will bypass the OCR and be processed by slower methods.

✎ Address location.

The last line of the address block (the OCR Read Area) must be at least $^5/_8''$ up from the bottom edge of the envelope, and the first line should be no more than $2^3/_4''$ from the bottom edge. Although the OCR accepts addresses within $^1/_2''$ from the left and right edges of the envelope, placing the address block approximately in the vertical and horizontal center is the norm. Be sure that no portion of the return address appears in the OCR Read Area.

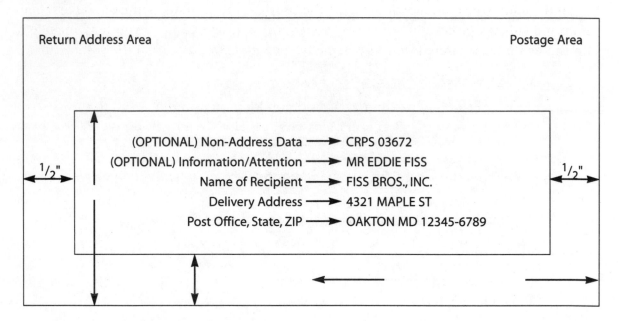

✎ Address characters.

Choose clear, readable type. Straight block lettering (such as Courier) is preferred, and individual letters must not touch or overlap. OCR allows for a character pitch of 7 to 12 characters per inch; 10 pitch is preferred. This means that no fewer than 7 and no more than 12 characters should fit into one inch of linear type. The height of each character must be no less than .08″ (about $^1/_{12}''$) and no more than .20″ ($^1/_5''$). A type size of 14 points is ideal.

Avoid unusual fonts (script, italic). Use black ink on a light (preferably white) background.

◻ Address format.

Place all non-address information, such as a coded data line, directly above the name and address of the recipient. Type all lines, single-spaced, flush with the left margin of the address block. All lines of the address should be parallel to the bottom of the envelope.

The Postal Service prefers that you use all caps, but lowercase letters in various type styles are acceptable provided they meet postal guidelines for OCR readability. When all caps are used, you may omit punctuation other than the hyphen in a ZIP+4 code. Instead, use one or two spaces to separate words; use two spaces between the two-letter state abbreviation and the ZIP code.

Type any special mailing notation (Certified Mail, Express Mail) below where the stamp or postage meter imprint will be. Type any on-arrival notation (Personal, Please Forward) on the left side of the envelope, about nine lines below the top edge. Do not type anything below the address block.

If the addressee is an individual, type the courtesy title and full name on the first line. If an individual's professional title is included in the inside address, you may include it on the first line, separated from the name by a comma, or place it on the second line.

<pre>
Ms. Penny Wise, Manager   Ms. Penny Wise
Hotel Suprema   Manager
                               Hotel Suprema
</pre>

If the addressee is a company or organization, type its full name on the first line and any department on the second line. If an attention line is used, place it directly above the street address.

<pre>
ABC Corporation
Sales Department
Attention Mr. I. O. Waugh
200 Business Circle
Louisville, KY 45555
</pre>

Type the full street address; include any unit designators (suite, apartment, floor, etc.) on the same line, separated by a comma. Abbreviate if necessary (see Appendix B, p. 156, for list of approved abbreviations).

<pre>
102 Main Street, Apt. 101 or 102 MAIN ST APT 101
</pre>

Place any information that will not fit in the street address line on the line *above* the street address.

<pre>
Suite 2690
50394 Peachtree Pavilion
</pre>

The last line of the address block includes the city, two-letter state abbreviation, and ZIP code (ZIP + 4, if known). Spell city names in their entirety unless space constraints require abbreviation. (See Appendix B, p. 156, for approved Postal Service abbreviations.)

NORTH HUNTINGTON HARBOR *becomes* N HUNTINGTON HBR

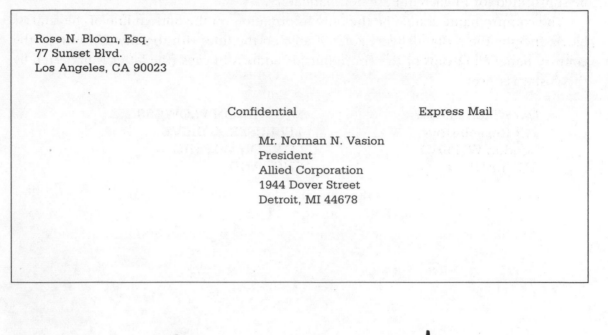

Rose N. Bloom, Esq.
77 Sunset Blvd.
Los Angeles, CA 90023

Confidential   Express Mail

Mr. Norman N. Vasion
President
Allied Corporation
1944 Dover Street
Detroit, MI 44678

⌂ Overseas addresses.

If possible, refer to the return address of previous correspondence for the correct ordering of the elements of an overseas address. Foreign courtesy titles (e.g., *Herr, Mme.*) may be substituted for English but are not mandatory.

The country name should be the only information on the bottom line of the address block. Include the postal delivery zone, if any, on the line with the city. Either type the country name all in caps or the entire outside address in caps (the latter is preferred by the Postal Service).

Mr. Wilton Flowers
117 Russell Drive
London W1P6HQ
ENGLAND

MR. WILTON FLOWERS
117 RUSSELL DRIVE
LONDON W1P6HQ
ENGLAND

Addressing individuals of unknown gender. See page 85.

4 Dear Sir or Madam

Social Titles and Salutations.... 84

When addressing women

When addressing individuals of
   unknown gender

When the addressee is unknown

When addressing couples

Problem Words................ 89

The word *man*

Masculine pronouns

Job titles and descriptions

4 Dear Sir or Madam

For generations, masculine terms have been used to indicate both sexes. Today, however, you will offend some recipients if you start a letter with *Dear Sir*, and many of your female readers will feel excluded if you write, "The effective salesman pays attention to his customers' needs."

Avoiding sexist terms is surprisingly easy. By following a few simple guidelines, you improve the likelihood of having a sympathetic audience—without resorting to awkward or silly language. A detailed exploration of sexist terms and their social implications is beyond the scope of *Better Letters*, but in this chapter we will review some basic ways to avoid gender bias in your letters. (For more extensive treatment of the subject, refer to "Resources for the Letter Writer," p. 182.)

SOCIAL TITLES AND SALUTATIONS

▢ When addressing women.

Many women want to be addressed either as *Ms.* or by their name without a title (Ms. Bertha Shipp, Bertha Shipp). Some women prefer *Mrs.*, either with their own first name or their husband's (Mrs. Hazel Nutt, Mrs. Saul T. Nutt). Still others (a minority today) prefer *Miss*.

Whenever such a preference is known, honor it. The easiest way to determine a preference is to notice how a woman signs her letters. If a preference is not known, either use *Ms.* or eliminate the social title.

Ms. Billie Dew
123 Main Street
Everytown, ND 59384

Dear Ms. Dew:

Billie Dew
123 Main Street
Everytown, ND 59384

Dear Billie Dew:

Academic or professional titles always take precedence over social or courtesy titles. Their nonsexist nature makes them especially useful.

Dr. Kara Lott
515 Independence Avenue
Centerville, IA 54321

Dear Dr. Lott:

Senator Lucie Cannon
U.S. Senate
Washington, DC 20510

Dear Senator Cannon:

When addressing individuals of unknown gender. _____

Some first names are given to both males and females (Leslie, Lee, Jan, Kim, Casey, Chris), while some women use initials when signing their names (E.Z. Wynn). In situations such as these where you may be uncertain about gender, using *Mr.* is no longer appropriate. Instead you might eliminate the social title and write the full name.

  Dear Bernie Sands: Dear N. E. Wonder:

Another option is to use the Simplified Letter format, which eliminates the salutation (see p. 52).

When the addressee is unknown. _____

The salutations *Dear Sir* or *Gentlemen* are a poor solution when you don't know your addressee's name. The more suitable *Dear Sir or Madam* and *Gentlemen and Ladies* are nonetheless cumbersome and somewhat offensive. *To Whom It May Concern* has an out-of-date flavor. The following paragraphs suggest a variety of alternatives for such out-moded salutations.

Generic Title. Certain categories of addressees lend themselves to grouping under a generic title.

Dear Homeowner   Dear Contributor

Dear Executive   Dear Parents

Dear Employee   Dear Solar Enthusiast

Dear Customer   Dear Supplier

Dear Union Member   Dear Reader

Job titles are sometimes used.

Dear Credit Manager

Dear Registrar

Dear Editor

Some people prefer to repeat the name of the company.

Dear Ten Speed Press

Dear General Motors

Dear Standard Pipe & Fixture Company

If you feel uneasy combining the word *Dear* with a company name or job title (after all, General Motors or Credit Managers are not "dear" to most people writing to them), consider the following alternatives.

Generalized Salutation. You can eliminate the word *Dear* by using a greeting you might exchange in person. *Good Morning* is a favorite with some writers but has the inherent drawback that it may not fit if the letter is read in the afternoon. *Good Day* gets around the time-of-day problem, but introduces Australian overtones that might distract the reader. *Hello* is popular with some but may seem too chummy to others. *Greetings* is suitable for many occasions when the addressee's name is unknown; however, the word has unpleasant connotations for many who have received draft notices.

If none of the suggested wordings seems exactly right, the best approach may be to eliminate the salutation altogether, as in Memos or the Simplified Letter.

Memos. Although memos have been used for internal company communication for years, many people now use them for a variety of correspondence. The memo is often the format of choice for e-mail. Headings of the typical memo are flush with the left margin, as follows:

To: Sales Manager, Arctic Ice Chest Company

From: Nifty Insulation, Inc.

Date: January 14, 2005

Subject: Improving Your Product

(Begin text here)

Simplified Letters. In many cases the Simplified Letter is the best solution when your addressee is unknown. It is more formal than a memo, while still eliminating the salutation. Here is an example of a letter written in the Simplified Letter format.

✓ Simplified Letter Format
✓ Request for Action

GOLIATH BROTHERS
79 Wall Street • New Utopia, WV 25000
Phone (200) 234-0987 • Fax (200) 987-4567

June 1, 2005

Holly Smoke
Smoke & Mirrors, Inc.
350 Hill Street, Suite 55
New Utopia, WV 25001

INSIDER TRADING

Recent criminal charges have focused national attention on investment bankers and other "insiders" who buy and sell stocks on the basis of proprietary information. As members of the New Utopia Stock Exchange, we must each police our own firm to wipe out this unethical--and illegal--practice.

The integrity of the entire industry is at stake. Clients are asking if we can be trusted with confidential information, and small investors see these cases as confirmation that the stock market is not for them.

We will be inviting unwanted government intervention if we are unable to control this practice. Self-regulation is the only solution. As a start, I urge you to adopt the measures suggested in the enclosed guidelines. Let me know your company's ideas for eliminating insider trading; I will include them in a follow-up letter next month.

Frank X. Change

FRANK X. CHANGE
PRESIDENT

✎ When addressing couples.

Today's letter writer confronts a variety of situations when addressing a couple. Many married women retain their own last name or adopt a hyphenated last name that combines their name with their husband's; some husbands hyphenate their name with their wife's name; unmarried couples live together. Each situation should be handled appropriately by the letter writer.

You have considerable latitude in the arrangement and order of names. Your safest course is to follow individual preferences when they are known and common sense otherwise.

If the husband's name has been taken, the traditional way to address the couple is:

Mr. and Mrs. Les Noyes
35 Opal Court
Cozy Village, MT 87943

Dear Mr. and Mrs. Noyes:

If the woman prefers to use her first name, the correct form of address would be:

Mr. Les and Mrs. Mary Noyes
35 Opal Court
Cozy Village, MT 87943

Dear Mr. and Mrs. Noyes:

If the woman has retained her maiden name, and both last names are relatively short, place the names on the same line:

Ms. Mary N. Haste and Mr. Les Noyes
35 Opal Court
Cozy Village, MT 87943

Dear Ms. Haste and Mr. Noyes:

If the last names are too long for one line, put them on separate lines:

Mr. Seymour Bearskin
Ms. Charlotte Moose
713 Trapper Way
Anchorage, AK 99703

Dear Mr. Bearskin and Ms. Moose:

Some etiquette authorities state that separate lines should also be used for the names of unmarried couples living together; others handle the names as they would a married couple when the wife has retained her maiden name.

The order of names is either alphabetical or arbitrary, depending on which authority you consult. Alphabetical order has the advantage of impartiality.

If a hyphenated name has been adopted, follow the usage of the individuals involved.

> Mr. and Mrs. William Aiken-Hart
>
> *or*
>
> Mr. William Hart and Mrs. Constance Aiken-Hart

(Cases where one or both individuals have professional titles are covered in Chapter 3, p. 65.)

PROBLEM WORDS

❒ The word *man.*

Man demonstrates the changes in meaning a word can undergo. The Old English meaning of the word was "person" or "human being," and it was applied to either sex. Thus someone's daughter or sister or mother could be described as "a dutiful man." Eventually the word *man* ceased to be used with regard to individual women; it became a term that distinguished adult males from adult females. At the same time, it continued to mean both sexes taken as a group, thereby producing some significant ambiguities.

A sentence I found in a handbook on writing illustrates both how the use of the word *man* can be troublesome today, and how easy it is to avoid the problem. The author made an introductory sort of "Bah! Humbug!" statement about how any reasonable person would understand that when he used words like *man* and *he*, he was not excluding women. Later in the book, however, he wrote the following sentence:

> The man who holds the chalk controls the meeting.

When you read this sentence, do you visualize a woman at the blackboard? I suspect not. Yet rewriting to avoid this bias is simplicity itself. Here are three ways to improve the offending sentence:

> The one who holds the chalk ...
>
> Whoever holds the chalk ...
>
> The person who holds the chalk ...

None of the alternatives is awkward, and they all allow the reader freedom in the choice of visual images.

Many women feel that using *man* as a word for people of both sexes relegates women to an invisible status. Even if you do not share this view, you will probably want to avoid muddying your meaning or alienating your reader. You have other ways to express the concept of both sexes.

Problem Word	Replacement
businessman	executive
chairman	chair, chairwoman, chairperson
congressman	congresswoman, member of Congress
councilman	councilwoman, council member
Englishmen, Frenchmen	the English, the French
layman, laymen	layperson, laypeople, laity
to man (verb), as in "to man the booth"	to staff, run, work, operate
man-hour	work-hour
mankind	humanity, human beings, civilization, the human race
manmade	artificial, synthetic, handmade, machine-made
manpower	personnel, staff, workers
repairman	service rep
salesman	saleswoman, sales rep, salesperson
workman	worker

Note: Words like *chairman* and *congressman* are appropriate when used in connection with a specific male.

The following pairs of sentences illustrate some common uses of the word *man* and suggest alternative wording. Notice how the ambiguity disappears when you don't have to guess whether *man* includes women.

Unemployment rates are meaningful to the average working man whose job may be on the line.

Unemployment rates are meaningful to the average worker (or wage earner) whose job may be on the line.

Pollsters rely on the opinion of the man in the street for their predictions.

Pollsters rely on the opinions of the average person (or voter) for their predictions.

Ancient man devised ways to observe the motions of the planets.

Our ancestors devised ways to observe the motions of the planets.

Man's creativity reveals itself in ...

Human creativity reveals itself in ...

Mankind owes to the child the best it has to give. —United Nations Declaration

Humanity (or The human race) owes to the child the best it has to give.

A common misunderstanding is that we should avoid not just the word but also the syllable *man*. This confusion created a national pastime a few years ago as people dreamed up outrageous substitutes. *Personeuver, personhole,* and *persondolin* were typical results of this exercise in absurdity.

But the syllable *man* is not always derived from the Old English word *man*. *Human* is from the Latin *humanus* (human being). Words such as *manipulate, manage, manufacture* and *manuscript* are derived from the Latin *manus* (hand); they have no roots in common with our word *man* and present no problems of ambiguity. We do not need substitutes for the syllable *man*, only for the generic noun.

▣ Masculine pronouns.

He, him, and *his* indicate a male person or the masculine possessive. If you wish to refer to females as well, you have several acceptable options:

- Change from singular to plural.
- Write in the second person.
- Revise to eliminate masculine pronouns.
- Use both pronouns.

Change from singular to plural. This allows you to use the neutral pronouns *they, them,* and *their*. The following quotations illustrate this approach; they appear first in their original form and then changed to plural.

> *Since a politician never believes what he says, he is always astonished when others do.* —Charles DeGaulle

> Since politicians never believe what they say, they are always astonished when others do.

An economist is an expert who will know tomorrow why the things he predicted yesterday didn't happen today. —Laurence J. Peter

Economists are experts who will know tomorrow why yesterday's predictions didn't come true today.

The plural noun *they* is sometimes used in singular constructions. Although this is grammatically incorrect, the trend indicates the widespread desire to avoid using masculine pronouns for both sexes.

It's enough to drive anyone out of their senses. —G. B. Shaw

My own preference is to avoid the ungrammatical mixing of singular and plural; I would probably wiggle out of the problem in Mr. Shaw's sentence by using the second person, as suggested below.

It's enough to drive you out of your senses.

Write in the second person. In some circumstances you can address the reader(s) as you (second person) rather than as the more anonymous he, she, or they (third person).

Change: When a man's friends begin to flatter him on how young he looks, it's a sure sign he's getting old.

to: *When your friends begin to flatter you on how young you look, it's a sure sign you're getting old.* —Mark Twain

Changing to the second person is particularly suitable with instructions. For example:

Change: Anyone wishing to receive a free subscription should enclose payment with his order. (third person)

to: If you wish to receive a free subscription, enclose payment with your order. (second person)

Revise to eliminate masculine pronouns. This is often the best solution when you have become bogged down with pronouns. The variety of ways we can express ourselves makes rewriting a relatively simple matter.

The tennis player must practice his serve...

The tennis player must practice serving...

The child who is afraid to go to bed by himself...

The child who is afraid to go to bed alone...

The consumer can stretch disposable income if he refrains from impulse buying.

The consumer can stretch disposable income by refraining from impulse buying.

Use both pronouns. If the plural form is not appropriate, you may prefer to write *he and she, her or his,* or *him or her.* In occasional use, the awkwardness of this construction is probably not a serious drawback. When you use it repeatedly, however, it develops a kind of *this or that, tit-for-tat* quality. Rewrite with some of the choices suggested above to avoid repeated pairing of pronouns.

Some writers address the problem by alternating masculine and feminine pronouns. This can be a bit disconcerting at first and should be used only as a last resort; however, most of us have come to accept such rotation if other ways around the problem are not workable. Writers who use feminine pronouns exclusively, presumably in an effort to correct the historical imbalance, convey a bias of their own that is not suitable for most correspondence.

🖉 Job titles and descriptions.

When men filled most of the jobs outside of the home and women's work was largely inside it, job titles incorporating the suffix *-man* were appropriate. In today's job market, few positions remain strictly male territory. Job titles and descriptions, including those with feminine endings (*-ess* or *-ette*), should be replaced by gender-neutral ones.

Recognizing the potential for gender discrimination with continued use of old-style titles, the U.S. Department of Labor has revised its system of occupational classification. The following examples from their *Job Title Revisions* indicate the nature of the changes.

Former Wording	Revised Wording
airline steward, stewardess	flight attendant
cameraman	camera operator
draftsman	drafter
flagman	flagger
foreman	supervisor
lineman	line installer, line repairer
maid	house worker
salesman	sales agent, sales associate
seamstress	sewer, mender
watchman	guard

Some of these revisions seem awkward, accustomed as we are to the old ways of expressing ourselves. But if you consider that a word like *salesperson* has been used for years without calling for comment, it may not be too farfetched to suggest that our ears will eventually accept such words as *businesspeople* or *spokesperson*.

The suffix *-er* can be a natural substitute for sexually biased terms such as draftsman (e.g., drafter). It has long been used in words like laborer, shopper, photographer, lawyer, runner, and writer. Is it any more difficult to say "repairer" than "explorer"? Most states have changed the term *workmen*, as in *workmen's compensation* to *worker (worker's compensation)* to reflect the trend toward neutral words.

Today, bias-free writing is habitual with many people—they don't have to give it much thought. The growing number of women in business suggests that you will want to avoid confusing or offending your reader by using biased terms. The fringe benefit is that nonsexist writing helps you communicate clearly and effectively.

5 Some Examples of Business Letters

Request for Action 98

Cover Letter 101

Sales Letter 103

Letter of Inquiry 112

Response to Inquiry 112

Complaint Letter 114

Response to Complaint Letter . . 117

Business Thank-You Letter 118

Collection Letter 119

Job-Related Letters 123

                    Resume Cover Letter

                    The Ineffective Cover Letter

                    Job Application Letter

                    Post-Interview Thank-You Letter

                    Letter of Recommendation

                    Letter of Resignation

5 Some Examples of Business Letters

A well-written letter conveys more about you than the specific information it contains. It tells your reader whether you are well-organized, thorough, and careful. A poorly written letter, on the other hand, sends the opposite message: You are sloppy, careless, and unwilling to take the time to do a good job.

A business letter represents you and your company. When it is read, you will not be present to correct false impressions or add missing information; for the moment, the words you put on the page have to serve as a stand-in for you. Those words mean business.

The first thing the recipient will notice is the appearance of the letter. To convey a professional image, the letter should be neat, error-free, and well placed on the page. (See Chapter 3, p. 48.)

Regard all letters as marketing tools, even though their primary purpose may be as a cover letter or a response to a complaint. Show consideration for your readers by not wasting their time with jargon or verbosity. (See Chapter 1, p. 18.)

The letters that follow are meant to suggest, not to prescribe. Use them to stimulate your own ideas for letters to your particular client, prospective employer, or delinquent account.

REQUEST FOR ACTION

Some letters ask a favor of the recipient or request action that takes time, effort, and maybe money. You will achieve the highest rate of response if your letters include the following:

1. a clear statement of the kind of information you are seeking;

2. a minimum number of questions, phrased so as to be easy to answer;

3. an explanation of why your reader would want to respond;

4. an expression of appreciation;

5. an addressed, postage-prepaid envelope.

Letter 1:

Some of our subscribers don't hesitate to tell us what they think of us. If an article offends or pleases them, we hear about it. But for every reader of *News & Views* who writes to us, thousands remain silent.

I would like to change that situation. We want to know what you like and don't like about our magazine: what interests you, which stories you wish we would cover, and which ones you would prefer we leave to our competitors.

To show our appreciation for your filling out our questionnaire, I enclose a pocket almanac. You will find it packs a great deal of useful information into a small amount of space—not unlike *News & Views*.

Thank you.

Letter 2:

Our computer recently flagged your account because it is missing some information required by the IRS. Please enter your Social Security number on the enclosed card and mail it to us today. Thank you.

Letter 3:

In order to qualify for tax-free sales, you must provide certain information about your store. Please fill out and return the enclosed resale tax card when you send us your check for Invoice No. 1492.

Thank you.

Donald Asher, author of numerous books on resumes, received the following letter from someone who failed to grasp the essentials of courtesy when requesting action. In my book, she qualifies for an "A" in effrontery.

Dear Mr. Asher: *(The letter-writer didn't even get his name right; it was addressed to David Asher rather than Donald Asher.)*

My name is _____. I am a Business Communications student at the Metropolitan Technical Community College in Omaha, Nebraska.

I have borrowed Resumes from College to Career from the library. Although I have not read your work yet one of my assignments is to write the author a letter. If I receive a response I will get an A for an extra credit grade.

I would greatly appreciate it if you would send a reply to my letter at your earliest convenience.

Sincerely,

W X Y Z

YOUR PUBLIC TELEVISION STATION

Post-Inquirer Building, Suite 42 / 345 Arch St. / St. Louis, Missouri 67834

Phone: (409) 555-9089 / Fax (409) 555-7654

July 8, 2005

N. E. Wan
One Chessboard Square
St. Louis, Missouri 67830

Dear Subscriber:

As a supporter of WXYZ, you'll be interested in the exciting programs we're planning for the fall:

• Sports enthusiasts can choose from programs on World Cup Soccer, tennis instruction, and Olympic retrospectives.

• Live television drama returns with the revival of Playhouse 100; some of our country's most talented actors will take part in this 25-week series.

• Film buffs will enjoy our continuing series of cinema classics, this year covering the decade from 1930 to 1940.

• A 12-part documentary on successful social programs will provide a refreshing counter-balance to the daily, and often depressing, news.

• The highly acclaimed children's series, Poppyseed Place, will present its twelfth year of educational fun.

In this brief letter, it's hard to suggest the broad scope of programs available on WXYZ. But it's not hard to know who makes them possible--subscribers like you! With your continued support, we will have another good season ahead. Please renew your subscription during the current pledge drive.

Thank you.

Sincerely yours,

Buck A. Nearing

Buck A. Nearing

P.S. If you send in your subscription in the next two weeks, we will send you a WXYZ tote bag. That's our way of saying a special "Thanks" for responding at this time.

COVER LETTER

A cover letter may have the sole purpose of identifying what is enclosed; it may also be designed to pique the interest of the recipient, and to highlight or expand on information in the enclosure. It can be one or two sentences long, or fill a whole page.

A sloppily written cover letter can sabotage your purpose—a point illustrated by a cover letter I received from an insurance agent. In the span of two short paragraphs, he left out an important word, repeated himself unnecessarily, and failed to notice that the closing "Sincerely" appeared both in the customary place and again below the enclosure notation. Although the agent presumably wanted my business, his sloppiness with a routine letter made me wonder if he was as careless when handling claims. Avoid sending such mixed messages. (See p. 123 for a discussion of cover letters that accompany a resume.)

The following cover letters range from short and simple identification of contents to a more fully developed sales tool.

Letter 1:

> I enclose a check for $49 for a one-year gift subscription to *Wired for Business.* Please send it to:
>
> > Otto Mann
> > 34 Gentrified Drive
> > Salt Lake City, UT 87654
>
> Thank you.

Letter 2:

> I enclose a brochure describing the NOW accounts that we discussed. As you can see, there are several advantages to having this type of account. The free services—safe deposit box, traveler's checks, notary—are probably the most important from your standpoint.
>
> I am happy to answer any further questions you might have and to assist you in transferring your account to the Main Street Bank.

Letter 3:

> The cost of heating or cooling a home is a significant part of the household budget. Inflation and higher energy prices have forced homeowners to choose heating and cooling equipment with care.
>
> The enclosed booklet describes state-of-the-art systems that you can install today. It compares the energy efficiencies of various models and indicates how soon they would pay back an investment by lowering your utility bills.
>
> This brochure is part of Consolidated Power Company's ongoing commitment to keeping our customers informed on energy-related matters. We welcome your comments or questions.

Furst and Foremost Management Consultants

3002 Market Street, Suite 507 / San Francisco, CA 94116
Phone: (415) 555-6745 / Fax (415) 555-7222

February 10, 2005

Mayor Nan O. Second
City of Los Angeles
City Hall
Los Angeles, CA 90123

Dear Mayor Second:

The enclosed proposal outlines our plan to improve employee productivity in your Parks and Recreation Department. Our program enables you to stretch both financial and human resources without laying off employees or reducing responsiveness to the public.

Mr. Ray Zinn will head our staff of specialists--a team that brings to this assignment a combined total of 50 years of experience in related fields. Mr. Zinn will report the team's findings to you each month during the one-year study.

In similar situations, Furst & Foremost has increased productivity 30 to 75 percent. We developed better communication between staff and management, and between department personnel and the public. The mechanisms we installed for airing grievances markedly improved employee morale.

You will find our program to be a powerful ally in tackling the problems of governmental cutbacks and inflationary pressures.

Very truly yours,

Hugo Furst

Hugo Furst, President

SALES LETTER

Sales letters are the lifeblood of most businesses. Many companies rely entirely on direct mail to bring in new customers, while others include letters as one part of a multifaceted marketing program. But few can conduct an effective sales effort without counting on letters to make potential buyers aware of their products.

To write a good sales letter, you should focus both on the product and on its market. Think carefully about how the product or service you are selling might appeal to a particular market.

✓ Simplified Letter Format
✓ Sales Letter

DOWNTOWN HEALTH CLUB
1001 Firm Butte
Tucson, AZ 80127

February 1, 2005

Mr. Jack N. Bachs
1495 Century Plaza, 11th Floor
Tucson, Arizona 80000

DOWNTOWN HEALTH CLUB OPENS

Have you ever noticed that people who survive a heart attack suddenly start watching their diet and getting exercise? There's a reason: Their bodies have sent them a powerful message.

Now, a heart attack is a compelling way to get your attention, but it's also a risky one. It's smart to get the message without the heart attack.

And the message is clear. Regular exercise and a sound diet improve the quality and length of our lives. We all know it, but many of us put off doing anything about it.

The new Downtown Health Club can change that. Our extended hours and convenient location allow complete flexibility in scheduling exercise breaks at any time of the day or evening.

And what does Downtown offer to members? State-of-the-art exercise rooms, a swimming pool, Jacuzzi, sauna, and handball courts. We have regularly scheduled classes and private instruction, as well as consultation with nutritionists and a follow-up Diet Watch. Truly a comprehensive program!

During the month of February, we're offering a free trial week to a few prospective members. We're sure that's all the time you will need to decide that the Downtown way to health and fitness works.

The enclosed brochure tells you more about our facilities and the various types of membership. Give us a try. You'll be doing your heart a favor.

DINAH SAWYER
VICE PRESIDENT, MEMBERSHIP

In some situations, not one but several letters may be needed to match the features of the product with the different kinds of buyers your letters will address. Each stresses the aspects you think would be of most interest to a particular type of customer. (See p. 36 for a discussion of how to analyze your readers.)

The following group of letters illustrates how you can "pitch" the same service—an insurance and financial services program—to different markets.

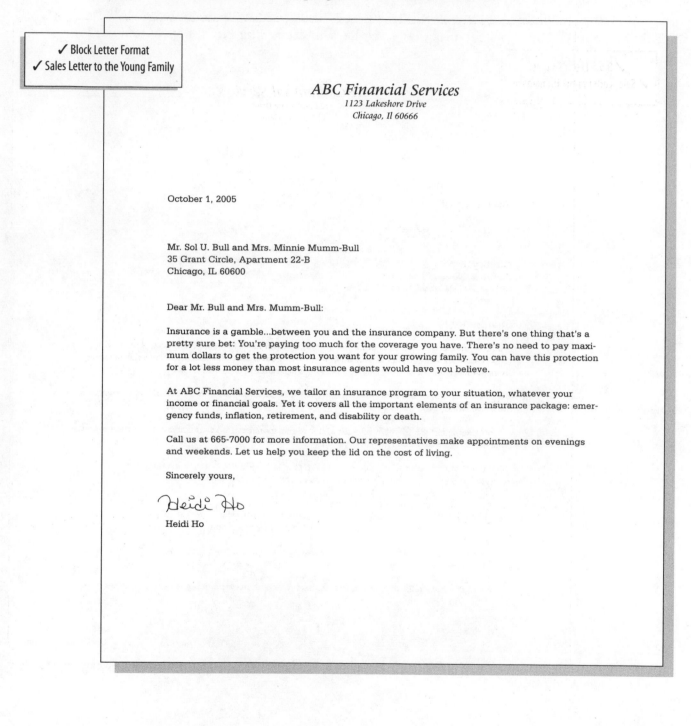

✓ Block Letter Format
✓ Sales Letter to the Young Family

ABC Financial Services
1123 Lakeshore Drive
Chicago, Il 60666

October 1, 2005

Mr. Sol U. Bull and Mrs. Minnie Mumm-Bull
35 Grant Circle, Apartment 22-B
Chicago, IL 60600

Dear Mr. Bull and Mrs. Mumm-Bull:

Insurance is a gamble...between you and the insurance company. But there's one thing that's a pretty sure bet: You're paying too much for the coverage you have. There's no need to pay maximum dollars to get the protection you want for your growing family. You can have this protection for a lot less money than most insurance agents would have you believe.

At ABC Financial Services, we tailor an insurance program to your situation, whatever your income or financial goals. Yet it covers all the important elements of an insurance package: emergency funds, inflation, retirement, and disability or death.

Call us at 665-7000 for more information. Our representatives make appointments on evenings and weekends. Let us help you keep the lid on the cost of living.

Sincerely yours,

Heidi Ho

Heidi Ho

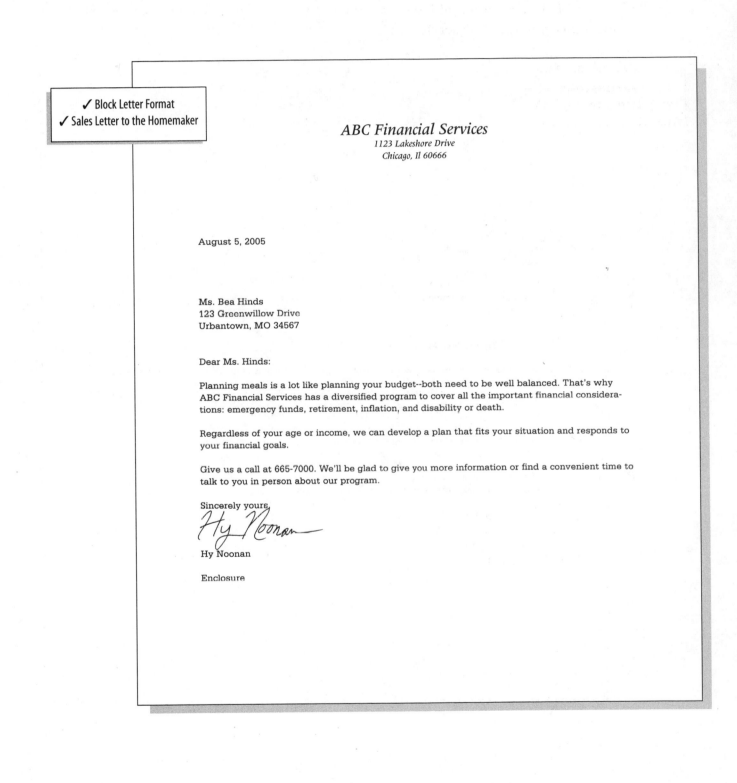

✓ Block Letter Format
✓ Sales Letter to the Homemaker

ABC Financial Services
1123 Lakeshore Drive
Chicago, Il 60666

August 5, 2005

Ms. Bea Hinds
123 Greenwillow Drive
Urbantown, MO 34567

Dear Ms. Hinds:

Planning meals is a lot like planning your budget--both need to be well balanced. That's why ABC Financial Services has a diversified program to cover all the important financial considerations: emergency funds, retirement, inflation, and disability or death.

Regardless of your age or income, we can develop a plan that fits your situation and responds to your financial goals.

Give us a call at 665-7000. We'll be glad to give you more information or find a convenient time to talk to you in person about our program.

Sincerely yours,

Hy Noonan

Hy Noonan

Enclosure

ABC Financial Services
1123 Lakeshore Drive

Chicago, Il 60666

September 15, 2005

Mr. and Mrs. Mack O'Roney
493 Primrose Path
Walker City, TN 37500

Dear Mr. and Mrs. O'Roney:

Insurance companies play the odds. But you don't have to do that in order to get maximum coverage at minimum cost.

Chances are, you're paying too much. At ABC Financial Services we will develop a financial program for your particular situation--whatever your income or goals. It will cost far less than your present program, while still covering the essentials:

GUARANTEED INCOME--Available for emergencies.

GROWTH--Putting your money to work to keep up with inflation.

PROTECTION--Financial support in the event of disability or death.

A call to 665-7000 is all that's needed to start you down the road to a sound financial future.

Sincerely yours,

Hap Hazzard

✓ Block Letter Format
✓ Sales Letter to the General Reader

ABC Financial Services
1123 Lakeshore Drive
Chicago, Il 60666

March 25, 2005

Mr. and Mrs. Bob A. Long
One Coast Road
Anybunk, ME 01234

Dear Mr. and Mrs. Long:

Does your nest egg keep getting nibbled?
Do you think you're too young to start planning for retirement?
Would major hospital bills or disability wipe you out?

If "Yes" is your answer to any of those questions, you should know about ABC Financial
Services.

We start where you are--whatever your age or income--and develop a financial plan that is surprisingly simple and inexpensive. Yet it covers all the major money problems you are likely to
encounter.

The enclosed brochure highlights some of the options available in our flexible plans. We would
be happy to provide more detail in person. Call us at 665-7000 to set up an appointment at your
convenience.

Very truly yours,

Homer Runn

Direct mail specialists claim that a four-page letter produces the best results. Based on my own reaction to the many four-pagers I receive, I'm not convinced. I first check the opening paragraphs to see if the product interests me, then skip to the last page in search of the price. (That's where it usually shows up.) I toss out any letter that makes it hard for me to locate the price. Only if a letter meets those two criteria (interest and price) do I read the middle pages.

Four-page letters do give you room to develop the merits of whatever you're selling. As an example, here's one I wrote to promote two of my books.

✓ Modified Block Format
✓ 4-pg Sales Letter

Periwinkle Press
P.O. Box 123
Mendowtown, CA 90123
(213) 355-9089, Fax (213) 342-1489

September 15, 2005

Mr. Wright A. Letter
Space, Inc.
One Techno Center, 35th Floor
World City, US 09876

Dear Mr. Letter:

Picture two individuals. Both are good at their jobs (marketing, public relations, personnel, research...), and both have just completed assignments that are to be reported to management.

One is comfortable with writing and prepares a concise, timely memo. The results of the assignment are clearly described, easy to grasp, and potentially useful. The other individual suffers from "writer's anxiety" and puts off writing the memo. When the report is finally submitted, it is poorly organized and its kernels of useful information are buried in stuffy jargon.

(1) Which person is more likely to get a raise?

(2) Which one is better about writing to her mother?

The answer to my first question is straightforward. People who write well usually do well. Few skills contribute more to success than the ability to write clearly and concisely.

My second question was a little test. Were you surprised, even just a bit, by the word "her"? Had you been assuming the individuals were men? The descriptions gave no clues as to their gender. I wrote them that way to illustrate, among other things, that bias-free writing is easy.

Good writing is important.
Writing skills and income often go together--and grow together. When you write well, your work looks better and you are a more effective employee, trainer, or manager. Good writing improves your chances of success.

✓ Modified Block Format
✓ 4-pg Sales Letter

Mr. Wright A. Letter, p. 2   September 15, 2005

Yet for many people, writing is the toughest part of their job. They flounder in circumlocutions and redundancies. They use state-of-the-art technology to write in an out-of-date style.

Help is at hand.
Write Right! and *Better Letters* were written for just such people. These books present the art of good writing in easily digested portions. Helpful during training sessions, indispensable as desk references, they are full of practical, down-to-earth information.

Write Right! and *Better Letters* can turn bad writers into good ones, and good writers into excellent ones. They are easy to use, thanks to their logical organization and meticulous indexing. The entertaining quotations that illustrate many of their rules make the books remarkably readable. For example:

"Put all your eggs in one basket—and watch that basket!"
—Mark Twain (to illustrate the dash)

"Scarce as truth is, the supply has always been in excess of demand."—Josh Billings (to illustrate the comma)

What is bad writing like—and does anyone care?
Bad writing uses too many words, has a stiff, legalistic style, and is usually in the passive voice. References are unclear, vague words leave readers wondering what the writer meant, and modifiers tacked on in the wrong place create confusion. The following examples illustrate bad writing, along with ways to effect repairs.

Too Many Words:
POOR: Our proposal follows the sequential itemization of points occurring elsewhere in your RFP wherever possible to facilitate your review.

BETTER: We will follow your outline.

Legalistic Style, Hackneyed Expressions:
POOR: Per our aforementioned discussion, I am enclosing herewith a copy of ...

BETTER: As promised, I enclose a copy of ...

Passive Voice:
POOR: It has been brought to our attention ...

BETTER: We noticed ...

✓ Modified Block Format
✓ 4-pg Sales Letter

Mr. Wright A. Letter, p. 3   September 15, 2005

Vague Words:
POOR: In view of domestic economic conditions ...

BETTER: With unemployment near ten percent ...

Misplaced Modifiers:
POOR: If you do not have a vehicle in which to store your food, please ask for assistance in
               hanging it from a Park Ranger.

BETTER: If you do not have a vehicle in which to store your food, please ask a Park Ranger for
               assistance in hanging it.

Unclear References:
POOR: This is the last year you can receive a 30% Solar Tax Credit for pools. Solar heat your
               pool now before it expires.

BETTER: This is the last year you can receive a 30% Solar Tax Credit for pools. Solar heat your
               pool now before the tax credit expires.

Sexist:
POOR: The consumer can stretch disposable income if he refrains from impulse buying.

BETTER: The consumer can stretch disposable income by refraining from impulse buying.

Does bad writing matter? You bet it does. Murphy's Law of Bad Writing says: "Anything that can
be misunderstood will be." Sloppy writing suggests that the writer is careless in other areas as
well, casting doubt on the writer's reliability. Instructions are not followed because readers are
confused. Time is wasted when readers must re-read in order to untangle the writer's meaning.
If the reading time for every memo could be shortened by as little as 30 seconds, it would save
hours every week and days every year.

What can be done to improve writing?

Here are some suggestions:

1. Write from an outline.
2. Avoid jargon.
3. Use the active voice.
4. Write with strong action verbs.
5. Use specific, concrete terms.

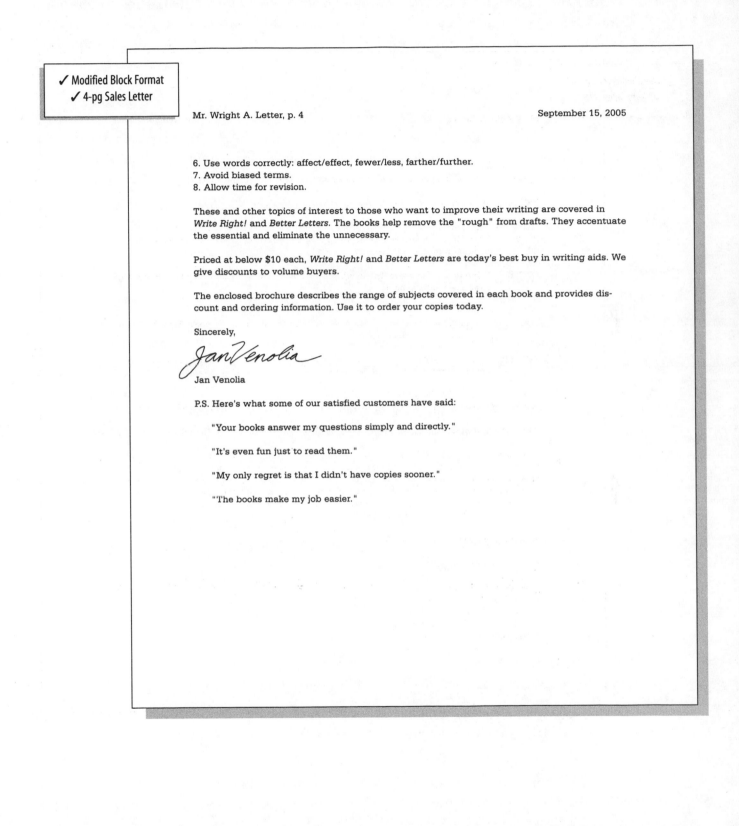

✓ Modified Block Format
✓ 4-pg Sales Letter

Mr. Wright A. Letter, p. 4   September 15, 2005

6. Use words correctly: affect/effect, fewer/less, farther/further.
7. Avoid biased terms.
8. Allow time for revision.

These and other topics of interest to those who want to improve their writing are covered in *Write Right!* and *Better Letters*. The books help remove the "rough" from drafts. They accentuate the essential and eliminate the unnecessary.

Priced at below $10 each, *Write Right!* and *Better Letters* are today's best buy in writing aids. We give discounts to volume buyers.

The enclosed brochure describes the range of subjects covered in each book and provides discount and ordering information. Use it to order your copies today.

Sincerely,

Jan Venolia

Jan Venolia

P.S. Here's what some of our satisfied customers have said:

"Your books answer my questions simply and directly."

"It's even fun just to read them."

"My only regret is that I didn't have copies sooner."

"The books make my job easier."

LETTER OF INQUIRY

Letters of inquiry must provide sufficient detail to obtain the desired action or information. If you are responding to an advertisement or other promotional medium, mention the name or source of your information. Be sure that your address is in the letterhead or body of the letter.

Letter 1:

> I read with interest the description of your research that appeared in the November issue of *Corporate Office.* Your ideas about the psychological effects of color and lighting are thought provoking, and since we plan to redecorate our offices soon, I would like to learn more about your findings.
>
> I would appreciate receiving a copy of the booklet, "Color and Light," which was mentioned in the article. Please send it to my attention at the above address.
>
> Thank you.

Letter 2:

> Please send me a copy of your current catalog and price list. I am planning to purchase a copier for my staff of six, and estimate our use at 500-1,000 copies per month.
>
> Eventually I will want to see various copiers demonstrated, but at this time I am only interested in receiving descriptive literature. I appreciate your help.

RESPONSE TO INQUIRY

When you respond to inquiries, whether spontaneous or solicited by some form of advertising, you write from a privileged position. You don't have to generate interest; your readers have already shown their interest by writing or phoning. This makes the job of promoting your products or services considerably easier.

Follow these steps to build on existing interest:

- Respond promptly.
- Spell names and addresses correctly.
- Set a friendly, positive tone without applying pressure.
- Provide all the information requested; if unable to do so, explain why.
- Make subsequent action by the potential customer easy.

Imagine yourself as the customer who knows nothing about the product or service. What information would you need to make a decision to buy? Emphasize those aspects you believe are of most interest to the recipient. Anticipate questions and answer them.

You can accomplish all these objectives with a well-written form letter, but be sure it doesn't *seem* like a form letter. Individualize it by changing a few words or adding a paragraph that addresses specifics of the inquiry.

✓ Modified Semiblock Format
✓ Response to Inquiry

Cozy Home Insulation
372 Warren Avenue
Tumbleweed Heights, OK 76113

May 9, 2005

Mr. Jay L. Warden
45 - 12th Street
Pulsa, OK 76543

Dear Mr. Warden:

The information you requested is contained in the enclosed booklet, "Home Insulation: Costs and Benefits." We are pleased to have this chance to spread the good news that you can cut heating bills by as much as one-half when you insulate your home properly. Even better, you and your family will be much more comfortable when your house is insulated with Insul-Star.

If you would like a cost estimate, we would be happy to drop by for a free consultation. Indicate the most convenient time on the enclosed postcard, or give us a call at 654-3210. As a service to working families, our estimators make appointments for weekday evenings and Saturdays from 9 to 1.

Thank you for your interest.

Sincerely yours,

Nan Tucket

Nan Tucket

COMPLAINT LETTER

When you are writing a complaint letter, you may be frustrated or angry, or both. But the person who first reads your letter will seldom be the one who created the problem; instead, that person is the one you want to help straighten it out. Thus, you should avoid accusations, threats, and sarcasm. If you have a legitimate complaint, simply presenting the facts will reveal it.

Include the following elements in a complaint letter:

1. A statement of the problem.

   "Our last shipment of printer ribbons was short one box."

2. The details needed for identification of the order or incident (date, model number, color, etc.).

   "I enclose a copy of the invoice which shows the type of ribbon and date of purchase."

3. The proposed corrective action.

   "Your customer service representative, Mrs. Pitt, indicated that we can receive either replacement ribbons or a credit to our account for the missing box. I prefer that you send replacement ribbons as soon as possible."

4. A positive closing, expressing confidence that your request will be met.

   "I appreciate your help in this matter. I have come to rely on the quality of XYZ products and on your service to customers.

✓ Modified Block Letter Format
✓ Complaint Letter

1395 Dartmouth Lane,
Apt. C
Evanston, IL 60500
April 1, 2005

Maxi-Mart Department Store
Accounts Payable
Center Shopping Mall
Evanston, IL 60501

Dear Computer:

I have never written a letter to a computer before, but it seemed the only appropriate action left. You and I are locked in an unending dance, the steps of which are roughly as follows:

(1) You write a letter stating that charges to my account at Maxi-Mart have exceeded the allowed limit. You request payment for the excess as well as the monthly balance due.

(2) I respond (letter dated 1/5/05) reporting that my December payment of $342.58 was never credited to my account, hence the problem. I offer to send a copy of the canceled check.

(3) Repeat of Step (1). Letter slightly more urgent.

(4) I respond (letter dated 2/15/05) and enclose a copy of both sides of my canceled check for payment of the December charges, which still have not been credited to my account.

(5) Repeat of Step (1). Letter borders on threatening.

Having failed to correct the situation with Steps (2) and (4), I am appealing to you directly (Step 6). It seems clear that I have taken all the necessary actions to confirm timely payment.

I hope my appeal convinces you or your operator to remove my name from your list of Bad Guys and restore it to your list of Good Guys.

Sincerely,

Peter Outt

Author's Note: Occasionally, a light touch is effective. I have addressed several letters to computers when conventional efforts have failed—it has worked every time.

✓ Block Letter Format
✓ Complaint Letter

MAYER & MAYER

2471 Catfish Jump Lane
Winsacula, MO 70321

July 24, 2005

Mr. Rob R. Barron, General Manager
Madisson Hotel
3299 Roman Holiday Court
La Toya, CA 92001

Dear Mr. Barron:

I would like to apprise you of a situation at your hotel that I believe needs correcting.

As a guest of the University of California, I was advised to stay at the Madisson specifically because it would save me (and the university) the cost of renting a car. I called your hotel, made a room reservation, and tried to make arrangements in advance for pickup at the airport. I was told not to worry about the pickup, and just to call when I arrived at the airport. I was led to believe that you had a courtesy bus that ran frequently, like other major hotels.

When I arrived at the airport last Friday afternoon, July 21, 2005, I could find no direct-line phone to the Madisson. I called your hotel from a pay phone and was told that the wait would be over an hour, and they couldn't even guarantee that! Mr. Barron, nobody staying in your hotel would find that acceptable.

When I protested that the very reason I was staying at the Madisson was because of the car service, I was told, "Well, Mr. Mayer, it is a courtesy van. You *could* take a taxi." I got the impression that the person booking your car appointments was insinuating that I was cheap and had no right to complain about a "free" service. I asked for other arrangements to be made to pick me up more quickly and was told that would be impossible. I asked for the Front Desk Manager, reached a gentleman named Kevin, told him my situation, and waited for him to suggest a solution. He did not.

I then canceled my reservation and told him I would notify the University that their arrangement with the Madisson was not working in the manner they had in mind. I rented a car and found a more convenient and more service-oriented hotel.

Mr. Barron, I know that you want to serve me as an individual guest, as well as all guests hosted by the University of California, but at this time your staff needs training and your service needs a thorough review. Here are a few suggestions:

1. Accept transportation reservations at the time of room booking.

2. Set and monitor minimum wait standards. When you cannot comply with those standards, offer taxi fare.

3. Install a direct-line telephone at the airport.

4. Train your staff to deal with customer complaints.

5. Empower your Front Desk Manager to solve these types of problems.

I hope you will find these suggestions useful.

Sincerely,

Mal D. Mayer

cc: Dean Molly Coddle
         University of California, San Diego

RESPONSE TO COMPLAINT LETTER

The public-relations function of letters that respond to complaints is of overarching importance. Even if the claim is unfounded, your job is to unruffle feathers and to keep the letter writer as a customer. Your response should include the following elements.

1. Acknowledge the problem up front.
   "Letters like yours provide valuable feedback. They let us know where we need to sharpen up our procedures."

2. Describe corrective actions.
   "A replacement for the defective part is on its way to you. I enclose a packet of discount coupons as a small compensation for your inconvenience."

3. Let the customer know you want their business.
   "We appreciate your business and look forward to serving you in years to come."

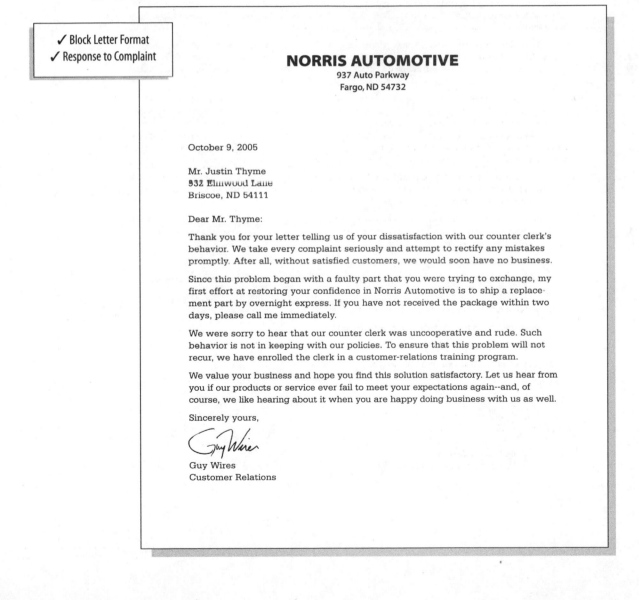

✓ Block Letter Format
✓ Response to Complaint

NORRIS AUTOMOTIVE
937 Auto Parkway
Fargo, ND 54732

October 9, 2005

Mr. Justin Thyme
932 Elmwood Lane
Briscoe, ND 54111

Dear Mr. Thyme:

Thank you for your letter telling us of your dissatisfaction with our counter clerk's behavior. We take every complaint seriously and attempt to rectify any mistakes promptly. After all, without satisfied customers, we would soon have no business.

Since this problem began with a faulty part that you were trying to exchange, my first effort at restoring your confidence in Norris Automotive is to ship a replacement part by overnight express. If you have not received the package within two days, please call me immediately.

We were sorry to hear that our counter clerk was uncooperative and rude. Such behavior is not in keeping with our policies. To ensure that this problem will not recur, we have enrolled the clerk in a customer-relations training program.

We value your business and hope you find this solution satisfactory. Let us hear from you if our products or service ever fail to meet your expectations again--and, of course, we like hearing about it when you are happy doing business with us as well.

Sincerely yours,

Guy Wires
Customer Relations

BUSINESS THANK-YOU LETTER

In business, as in personal matters, expressions of appreciation are always welcome. Even a short note of thanks maintains and strengthens relations. And yet, thank-you letters are a neglected form of communication. Develop the habit of writing thank-you notes; it is one of the best ways to apply your letter-writing skills.

✓ Modified Block Format
✓ Business Thank-You

WIDGETRON AMALGAMATED
2973 Evergreen Terrace
Seattle, WA 98771

March 29, 2005

Dr. Steffi Scope
350 Lakeside Drive
Spokane, WA 98765

Dear Dr. Scope:

Thank you for the lunchtime seminar on Fun in the Workplace which you gave to our management team yesterday. Your presentation was both informative and lively, and we found your examples particularly relevant to the challenges of our consulting business.

We have already instituted several of the principles you covered and plan to phase in some of the more extensive programs in the months ahead. We look forward to inviting you back in six months to assess our progress and to inspire us once again.

Yours truly,

Sue Venier

Sue Venier

COLLECTION LETTER

Collection letters are sent to customers who haven't paid their bills. Such letters are often referred to as the "collection series," because more than one letter is often needed to accomplish the objective. The letters move from gentle reminders to heavy artillery. Yet each letter must be written as if you expect it to be the last, as if this is the one that will do the trick.

Collection letters perform more than one function. In addition to their primary purpose of collecting overdue accounts, they are an important sales tool. In fact, the effective collection letter has much in common with the sales letter; it sells the customer the idea of paying the bill—and even of continuing to do business with your company.

In most cases, you want to retain the business of the overdue account. But even if you would prefer never to deal with this customer again, you stand the best chance of collecting the amount due if you avoid words that irritate or antagonize. A genuinely disgruntled customer can lead to the loss of more than one account.

Collection letters should reveal an understanding of the customer's position (the "you" attitude); the accusatory tone of "me *vs.* you" is unproductive. At first, assume the customer wants to pay and just needs a little reminding. But even early reminders should not have the appearance or flavor of a form letter; they should read and look as if they were directed right at the reader. Customers who sense that they have received a form letter may be encouraged to delay payment a little longer. You send signals of not yet taking a real interest in the case if your letter smacks of "Letter-B-2: Delinquent Accounts, 30-60 days."

Timing is important. The interval between letters should allow for a response and for the possibility that the recipient is ill or out of town. The customer's credit rating will also influence timing. Those with an excellent rating should be allowed a liberal amount of time between letters, while those with a record of slow payment or a poor credit rating would probably receive more frequent notices with a stronger tone.

Always leave the reader with precise instructions. Don't present mixed alternatives, such as the following:

> A weekly payment of $50 will clean up your balance. If that's too much, send $35 each week—or start with $20 if that's all you can manage. Just let us know what you plan to do.

Presented with such a confused request, the recipient will probably do none of them.

The first collection letter should be sent after the customer has received the original invoice and a follow-up statement; here you simply draw attention to the overdue amount in a friendly tone. In the letter that follows, you can inquire about whether there is a reason for the delay—something lost in the mail, an error in the records, or possibly dissatisfaction with the goods or service.

The next letter in the series assumes that the previous assumption was mistaken and that, in fact, the customer is deliberately delinquent. At this point you appeal to the customer's sense of responsibility and fair play as well as to self-interest (e.g., avoiding late charges, protecting credit rating). You indicate the company's desire to help solve the problem, while making it clear that your ability to help delinquent clients has its limits. If you approach these letters with a light touch, using humor or even a gimmick to attract attention, your chance of success will be improved. L. E. Frailey illustrates the art of using humor in *A Handbook of Business Letters* (see "Resources for the Letter Writer," p. 182).

> Once when Lincoln was poor and hungry, a stranger approached him and requested change for a $20 bill.
>
> Being without a cent, and seeing the humor of the situation, Lincoln stooped down and confided: "Sorry, I can't oblige you, stranger, but I thank you for the compliment just the same."
>
> Some of our friends pay us the same compliment that the stranger paid Lincoln. They let their account stand on the books, thinking no doubt that we don't need the money. But we do. You would be surprised.

The final letter in the series assumes that the customer will pay only if forced to do so. The threats you employ depend on how you intend to pursue the matter. If you plan to turn the case over to a collection agency or an attorney, make it clear that the customer can still avert this drastic action—with its high costs to *all* parties—by acting before a certain date. Do not make empty threats; advise the customer only of those actions you will actually take. You may wish to write the final-stage letter to be signed by a high-level company official.

A series of collection letters might progress as follows:

Letter 1:

> Your account, with a past-due balance of $498.75, has just appeared in my "tickle file." That indicates it's time to tickle your memory with a reminder that you owe us some money.
>
> If you have already mailed your check, please accept my thanks. We look forward to being able to serve you again.

Letter 2:

> There is probably a good reason why you haven't answered our inquiry about your overdue account. Sometimes a statement is misfiled, a check is lost in the mail, or there is an error in our records. Whatever the source of the problem, we are in the dark until we hear from you.

We have two reasons for wanting a response. Obviously, we want to be paid. But just as important, we want you to feel free to reorder. By clearing the $498.75 due, you will allow us to continue sending you the supplies you need, as you need them. That will help your sales—and ours. Why not check your inventory and use the enclosed envelope to send an order with your payment?

Letter 3:

Your company and ours may have something in common: a cash-flow problem. In our case, the problem comes from customers who don't pay their bills. Is that the source of your difficulty, too? The ripple effect from slow-paying customers makes us realize how we are all in this boat together; when each of us does our share of the rowing, it helps everyone to get ashore.

Your past-due balance is $498.75. If special circumstances make complete payment impossible, let's get together and work out a schedule of reduced installments. You have been a valued customer, and we want to keep it that way.

Letter 4:

When all else fails, you drop back 20 and punt. That pretty well describes our situation. You have not answered our previous letters reminding you of your now long-past-due balance of $498.75.

This leaves us no alternative but to "punt," by referring your account to the Friendly Collection Agency. We consider this a drastic step, so we are writing one more time to ask your cooperation. If we hear from you by May 10th, you will keep us from taking action we would rather avoid. You will also protect your good name.

Creditors have better memories than debtors.
—Benjamin Franklin

RAINBOW GLASS AND MIRROR CO.

300 Cortland Avenue   Sacramento, California 90987   (203) 456-0987

Mr. Lionel Train
Train Toys, Inc.
140 Lathrop Avenue
Lathrop, Kentucky 48000

Dear Mr. Train:

Thank you for your prompt response to our request for payment of Invoice No. 7304. We reviewed our books and bank deposits once again to see if your check was incorrectly entered but could find no record of it.

By now the bank should have returned the canceled check to you. Will you please send us a photocopy of both sides? I enclose a self-addressed, stamped envelope for your convenience.

If you are unable to find the canceled check, then we must assume your payment was lost in the mail. In that case, please use the enclosed envelope to send us a new check.

I appreciate your help in resolving this matter.

Sincerely yours,

Mardi Graw

Mardi Graw
Controller

dkf

Enclosure: Envelope

JOB-RELATED LETTERS

▣ Resume cover letter.

Always send a cover letter when you submit a resume—it's what will make all the effort you put into crafting the resume pay off. Typically, the recipient will glance at a resume and then go back to read the cover letter before deciding whether to devote more time to the resume. So don't fail to give this letter its due.

The first step is to clarify your thinking. What do you want? What do you have to offer? Move into the prospective employer's shoes, examining your background not from the standpoint of "This is what I have done," but "Here is how I can help you."

Make a list of your accomplishments, using action verbs to describe them (see Appendix A, p. 153). If possible, show the results of what you did, not a laundry list of activities or job functions. For example:

> **Achieved 15% capture rate on proposals to business and government clients.**
>
> **Inaugurated and directed a marketing contact scheme that doubled our list of active customers.**

Your letter must be error-free—no misspelled words, no glaring errors in punctuation or usage. Deliver on any promises you make (e.g., "I will phone next week").

The following suggestions draw upon advice found in *The Damn Good Resume Guide* (see "Resources for the Letter Writer," p. 182).

1. Address someone in authority by name and title. Be sure you spell the name correctly.

2. Tell how you became attracted to this particular company.

3. Demonstrate that you've done some homework on the company and can see THEIR point of view (their problems, interests, priorities).

4. Convey your enthusiasm for and commitment to this line of work.

5. Balance professionalism with personal warmth and friendliness. Avoid the stilted language often found in business letters (see p. 8).

6. Describe at least one thing about you that's unique—say, a special gift for getting along with all kinds of people—something that goes beyond the basic requirements of the position, that distinguishes you, *and* is relevant to the position.

7. Be appropriate to the field you're exploring; stand out, but in a non-gimmicky way.

8. Identify specifically what you are seeking as well as what you are offering.

9. Point directly to the next step, telling just what you will do to follow through.

10. Be as brief and focused as possible.

✓ Modified Block Letter Format
✓ Resume Cover Letter

279 College Avenue
Boulder, CO 800210
March 5, 2005

Ms. Constance Comment, President
ADVENTURE Clothing Design
Central Tower, 10th Floor
Denver, CO 80200

Dear Ms. Comment:

When I visited ADVENTURE Headquarters yesterday, I was impressed by the exceptional workplace environment you have created. I had read of your company's innovative approach to
encouraging employee feedback and participation, but it was exciting to see it in action. The
atmosphere fairly crackled with energy and ideas.

My enthusiasm and years of experience would be useful to ADVENTURE. I have a good color
sense, I'm sensitive to developing trends, and I know the importance of coordinating fabrics and
accessories. I have been a buyer of women's clothing for Brandhoff's Department Stores for the
past five years and have a degree in Business Administration from Denver College. The enclosed
resume provides additional details of my background.

I would like to meet you to discuss how my skills could benefit ADVENTURE. I will phone next
week to see if we can find a convenient time.

Sincerely yours,

Hope Springs

▣ The ineffective cover letter.

Sometimes it helps to know not only what works but what doesn't work. In their book, *Dynamic Cover Letters,* Katherine and Randall Hansen list a dozen common qualities that can keep a cover letter from attracting the right kind of attention. Their points are abstracted here; for further discussion and illustration, I recommend the Hansens' book. (See "Resources for the Letter Writer," p. 182.)

An ineffective cover letter has the following shortcomings:

1. A boring and formulaic opening paragraph.

2. Lengthy, uninteresting paragraphs, or a total length of more than one page.

3. An autobiographical tone, rather than a sales pitch that inspires the employer to set up an interview.

4. Diluting its impact with phrases such as "I think" or "I feel."

5. Requesting an entry-level job; that may be what you are qualified for, but why sound as if you lack ambition?

6. Unsubstantiated value judgments (back them up by correctly attributing them to past employers or professors).

7. Dwelling on what the employer can do for you, instead of what you can do for the employer.

8. An unsolicited salary request.

9. Unnecessary negative information.

10. A desperate tone, as if you are willing to do anything.

11. Ignorance of the company to which you are writing.

12. Sounding wimpy or passive about your experience. Say "I took the opportunity," not "I was given the opportunity."

▣ Job application letter.

The letter you write seeking a job might be in response to a known opening, or it might be a "fishing expedition." Either way, it could be the most important letter you write. Letters produce interviews which produce jobs.

About 500 pieces of paper cross the desk of the average busy executive each week. If one-fourth of the workday is devoted to reading correspondence, that amounts to about one minute each. You may have only a few seconds to grab someone's attention.

Include only enough information to arouse interest in your qualifications. The goal of the letter is to obtain an interview, during which you can provide additional details. The following letter includes some resume-type information, but does not attempt to replace the resume.

Ames Hyer

606 Palm Street, Coral Gables, Florida 30090
(303) 999-8712 / Fax (303) 999-2386

May 15, 2005

Mr. Al Ligori, Manager
Personnel Department
MegaCity Manufacturing, Inc.
1550 Industrial Parkway
Cleveland, Ohio 45555

Dear Mr. Ligori:

Today's Tribune announces a job opening in your Marketing Department. The initiative and enthusiasm I would bring to such a position will be of interest to you.

In my ten years in sales, I have demonstrated an unusual ability to find new markets and to develop novel applications for existing products. For example:

-I inaugurated and supervised a complete direct mail program, including preparation of the mailing pieces, selection of the mailing list, and analysis of the returns. The exceptional 5% response rate made direct mail a standard part of the company's marketing plans.

-I developed the market for a line of books in quick-print shops; the high sales volume resulting from the close match between books and shop clientele led to nationwide distribution through several printshop franchises.

-I supervised the design and staffing of a trade show booth that produced nearly twice as many sales leads as previous trade shows.

No letter can adequately convey an individual's talents. If my background matches the qualifications you are seeking, I feel certain that a personal interview would be worthwhile.

Very truly yours,

Ames Hyer

Ames Hyer

If you have only limited job experience, or none at all, consider what you *do* have to offer a potential employer. With a little imagination you may find you have just what an employer needs. For example:

✓ Modified Block Letter Format
✓ Job Application Letter

234 Fourth Street, Apt. C
Suntown, AZ 87654
July 20, 2005

Dr. Mal Practiss
Medical Mall, Suite 5F
356 Appletree Street
Madison, Wisconsin 56789

Dear Dr. Practiss:

Personnel turnover is often a problem in medical offices. That's why you will be interested in my background in hospital record-keeping--and my tenacity.

I have worked more than 5,000 hours as a volunteer at Harbor Hospital. My responsibilities included bookkeeping for the hospital gift shop (paying suppliers, recording sales, and transferring profits monthly to the hospital), and sorting over 600 pieces of patient mail each week.

I have a working knowledge of the forms required by insurance companies and by Medicare, based on assistance I have rendered to my elderly parents and to a number of their friends.

My interest in working in a doctor's office has prompted me to study medical terminology on my own. If part of your employee screening procedures includes testing in this area, you will find that I have pursued my studies effectively.

My family-raising years are now behind me, and I am looking forward to several productive decades in medical office work. I would be pleased to meet with you to discuss how I could provide the kind of help you are seeking. My phone number is 406-0298.

Sincerely yours,

Meg Olopolis

Meg Olopolis

❏ Post-interview thank-you.

A follow-up letter after a job interview will make you stand out as thoughtful, businesslike, and interested in the job. Address your letter to the person who interviewed you (spell his or her name correctly), and refer to the date of the interview and the position desired.

Take this opportunity to underscore any strong features of the interview, your responses to new information about the job or company that arose during the interview, and your updated view of how you could fit into the company.

✓ Modified Semiblock Format
✓ Post-Interview Thank-You

123 Third St., Apt. 125
Las Vegas, Nevada 89015
June 3, 2005

Ms. Roxanne Stones
XXX Company
5930 Highland Avenue
Las Vegas, Nevada 89012

Dear Ms. Stones:

Thank you for arranging such an informative meeting yesterday. Our interview confirmed my sense that my background in hazardous materials would be useful to the XXX Company.

As we discussed, community relations are an often neglected aspect of toxic waste disposal, and the "people skills" I have developed in my years with the EPA would assure adequate airing of the views of everyone concerned.

I appreciated the opportunity to talk with Dr. Smith and Ms. Jones. Clearly you have a knowledgeable and enthusiastic staff working with you. My thanks to all of you for taking the time to meet with me.

I look forward to learning of your decision.

Sincerely yours,

Marva Less

Marva Less

❏ Letter of recommendation.

When you write a letter recommending a friend or employee for a job, include the following information:

- how long you have known the individual,

- the nature of your acquaintance or relationship (e.g., supervisor, class-mate),
- your evaluation of the individual's qualifications for the particular job (if known).

Incidentally, when writing the letter, consider that it may one day be read by the person it describes.

The amount of detail you provide will reveal your level of enthusiasm about the candidate; a few generalized statements suggest a satisfactory performance, but paragraphs of meaningful description indicate that you believe the candidate possesses superior qualifications.

The following letters are strong recommendations.

✓ Block Letter Format
✓ Letter of Recommendation

Deep Six Marine Resarch
5391 Davy Jones Boulevard
Santa Barbara, CA 93107

November 1, 2005

Dr. Marshall Arts
Graduate Admissions
University of the World
Mail Drop B-25
Collegeville, UT 87654

Dear Dr. Arts:

Dee Nye has worked directly under my supervision for the past five years. Her assignments concerning the geophysics and chemistry of manganese nodules called for a grasp of fundamental principles as well as meticulous attention to detail. She proved to be industrious, conscientious, and skillful in carrying out her assignments.

Ms. Nye developed software that expedited conversion of raw data into useful form; she calibrated our sedimentometer and used it to measure systems of interest. She has had experience in zonal rotor work on the Epson B-2000 ultracentrifuge and has used the Ellery 21 spectrophotometer extensively. Her recent work in electron microscopy stimulated a new line of research.

Ms. Nye brings to her work a high degree of integrity and a cheerful personality. Her intellectual vigor and the tenacity with which she has pursued problems in our laboratory suggest that she is well qualified to enter a program leading to the Ph.D. degree.

Very truly yours,

Dulcie Murr

Dulcie Murr, Ph.D.

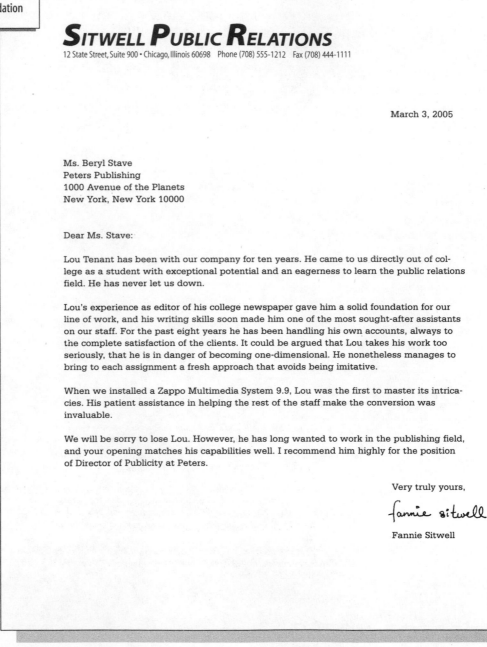

✓ Modified Block Letter Format
✓ Letter of Recommendation

SITWELL PUBLIC RELATIONS

12 State Street, Suite 900 • Chicago, Illinois 60698   Phone (708) 555-1212   Fax (708) 444-1111

March 3, 2005

Ms. Beryl Stave
Peters Publishing
1000 Avenue of the Planets
New York, New York 10000

Dear Ms. Stave:

Lou Tenant has been with our company for ten years. He came to us directly out of college as a student with exceptional potential and an eagerness to learn the public relations field. He has never let us down.

Lou's experience as editor of his college newspaper gave him a solid foundation for our line of work, and his writing skills soon made him one of the most sought-after assistants on our staff. For the past eight years he has been handling his own accounts, always to the complete satisfaction of the clients. It could be argued that Lou takes his work too seriously, that he is in danger of becoming one-dimensional. He nonetheless manages to bring to each assignment a fresh approach that avoids being imitative.

When we installed a Zappo Multimedia System 9.9, Lou was the first to master its intricacies. His patient assistance in helping the rest of the staff make the conversion was invaluable.

We will be sorry to lose Lou. However, he has long wanted to work in the publishing field, and your opening matches his capabilities well. I recommend him highly for the position of Director of Publicity at Peters.

Very truly yours,

Fannie Sitwell

Fannie Sitwell

⬭ Letter of resignation.

Accepting a new position, job dissatisfaction, and retirement are circumstances that typically call for a letter of resignation. Often such letters merely document an event that has been expected or discussed by all parties. A single sentence may suffice for this situation:

> **Please accept my resignation, effective November 1, 2005.**

However, you may wish to include information or express sentiments beyond this bare-bones statement. Let the function of the letter determine its tone and content.

Usually you will want to maintain strong ties with the company you are leaving, so make your letter friendly. On the other hand, you may wish to use your letter as the means of documenting grievances. But even if you intend to send the letter to the newspaper in order to draw attention to a particular circumstance, an objective tone is appropriate.

✓ Block Letter Format
✓ Letter of Resignation

Anne T. Frieze
4044 Sunrise Street, Miami, FL 33014

July 1, 2005

Don Keyes, District Attorney
Broward County
One Courthouse Square
Miami, FL 33333

Dear Mr. Keyes:

With this letter I am resigning my position as Deputy District Attorney, effective immediately. In the eight years I have served as prosecutor, I have attempted to address the imbalance of our system of justice which favors the criminal over the victim. While you and I differ on the role of the District Attorney's office, I have appreciated the open way you have discussed this matter with me. I also understand that the department budget is largely out of your hands since it is determined by the Board of Supervisors.

It is therefore with regret that I conclude I can no longer function as a prosecutor under administration policies that fail to provide the investigative support I need in order to obtain convictions.

Very truly yours,

Anne T. Frieze

✓ Modified Block Letter Format
✓ Letter of Resignation

March 28, 1912

Sir Izzy Reel, Chairman
White Star Steamship Company
Pier 37
Liverpool, England

Dear Sir Reel:

This letter puts into writing the resignation I regretfully submitted to you in person yester-day. I feel the greatest loyalty to the company and wish to express my gratitude for the encouragement given to me throughout the years of my advancement from Cabin Boy to Chief Engineer.

As you know, I had planned to retire following my next tour of duty at sea. However, the personal circumstances we discussed make it impossible for me to assume those duties when the ship sails next week. It therefore seems appropriate to move the date of retire-ment forward to April 1, 1912, to correspond with the present situation.

My regret concerning this action is all the stronger for my being unable to participate in the maiden voyage of the newest in a long line of illustrious passenger ships. I had been look-ing forward to having my final tour on "the engineering marvel of the century." Although I will be unable to be on board, my spirit will be with the Titanic when she sails from Liverpool next week.

With my sincere thanks,

U.R. Thayer

(*Author's Note to History Buffs*: The above letter is entirely fictitious.)

Travel letters. See page 140.

6 Some Examples of Personal Letters

Handwritten or Typed?........137

Letters to Family and Friends...137

Thank-You Notes

Keeping in Touch

Travel

To Your Children

Sympathy

Response to a Sympathy Letter

As Consumer and Citizen.......143

Complaint Letter

Letter to Government Representative

Soliciting Funds

6 Some Examples of Personal Letters

Think of what a lift it gives you to see a letter from a friend or relative in the stack of bills and junk mail. Yet even though we all like to receive those letters, few of us write them; it seems so much easier to pick up the phone. As a result, personal letters are in danger of going the way of the buggy whip and the dodo bird.

Lack of time is the excuse many people use for not writing, but often they are just not comfortable putting words on paper. My goal in this chapter is to overcome such resistance. If we follow the Golden Rule of Letter Writing, we will write letters because we like to receive them. Besides, letters remain the best way to conduct personal affairs in many situations. Letters allow us to

- express thanks or sympathy,
- make views known to elected officials,
- register a complaint,
- share experiences,
- maintain friendships and family ties over long distances.

A letter is an excellent way to express your feelings. When a friend experiences a death in the family or is seriously ill, a letter is one of the most meaningful ways to show that you care. Sharing happy occasions is equally important: the joy of becoming a grandparent, the excitement of travel, the fun of a class reunion. The contacts we maintain through letters can be a haven in an impersonal world.

Letters help you fulfill your responsibilities as citizen and consumer. The individually written letter is more powerful than ever because, alas, so few people write them nowadays. True, elected officials are flooded with mail, but the bulk of it is form letters cranked out by interest groups. A letter that expresses original thoughts and sentiments will receive special attention. Similarly, a letter to a company protesting their advertising policy, for example, can make a difference; a letter to a newspaper editor clearly stating your views will probably be printed. Well-written letters make people sit up and take notice.

This chapter includes examples of the kinds of letters you might want to write. They are suggestions for the form or spirit of specific types of letters, not formulas to be followed. Your own thoughts will provide more appropriate words for a given situation. The key ingredient is the sincerity with which you express yourself.

…more than kisses, letters mingle souls, for thus friends absent speak.
—JOHN DONNE

HANDWRITTEN OR TYPED?

The most personal of letters, such as letters of sympathy, congratulations, and thanks, should always be handwritten. Letters to newspaper editors or companies will probably produce the best results if they are typed. If you have good, legible handwriting, you may want to handwrite letters to elected officials in order to drive home the point that your letter was not mass-produced. However, if you want to take advantage of the efficiency of a word processor to send the same letter to several people (or if your handwriting is illegible), go right ahead and type them. You overcome the impersonal appearance of a typed letter by adding a brief handwritten postscript.

Typing a letter to a friend is now considered socially acceptable. Family members will receive more news in less of your time if you type letters to them. But if your mood is more suited to curling up with pen and paper than sitting down to a keyboard, by all means write by hand. The more you enjoy the letter-writing process, the better your letter will be.

LETTERS TO FAMILY AND FRIENDS

The format of personal letters is quite simple. Put the date near the top of the page, usually on the right side; omit an inside address. Place a comma following the salutation, instead of the colon used in business letters. Indent paragraphs about an inch, if handwritten, or five spaces, if typed. Try to avoid dividing words at the end of lines. Place the complimentary close and your signature slightly to the right of center. That's about all there is to it.

▣ Thank-you notes.

Letters saying "Thank you" should be written upon many occasions: when you receive a gift or are someone's guest; when you have been granted an interview; when a friend or colleague has written a reference for you. Any time you have been the beneficiary of someone's hospitality, generosity, or willingness to help, a note of thanks is appropriate.

The letter should be written promptly; the sincerity of your appreciation is diminished by allowing a long interval to elapse. The letter need not be lengthy. My mother used to call thank-you notes "bread-and-butter letters," presumably because your bread and butter sometimes depended on how well you maintained your personal ties. Here's an example of the kind of letter my mother trained her children to write; it would be just as suitable today as it was then.

April 25, 2005

Dear Tom and Jerri,

    My visit to Chicago was a memorable occasion, made all the more so by your thoughtful hospitality. You certainly know how to make a guest feel at home! Your delicious meals were a treat, and your flexibility in adapting to my irregular schedule helped me get more done than I had imagined possible.

    Plan on staying with me if your travels bring you to New England. I will look forward to more hours of stimulating discussion—and just plain fun.

                  Best regards,

Buying a commercial thank-you card is never as satisfactory a way of expressing appreciation as a few handwritten sentences. The original sentiments you convey count for a lot more than those dreamed up by employees of a greeting card company.

July 10, 2005

Dear Aunt Vi and Uncle Clem,

Diane and I appreciate your thoughtful choice of wedding present. The salad bowl will not only be useful, but it's a real beauty as well.

We're working hard on our long-hidden talents as gourmet cooks, and the bowl will be great to have for our culinary creations.

Thanks from both of us!

                  Love,

~

June 15, 2005

Dear Grandma and Grandpa,

The dictionary you sent arrived today, just two days before graduation. Spelling has always been my Waterloo—you can be sure the dictionary will see a great deal of use when I get to college.

Thanks for picking out such a helpful gift.

                  Love,

Even when you are not particularly thrilled with a gift, a brief note is in order. If you keep in mind that the gift was sent with the best of intentions, you can probably find something suitable to say.

May 25, 2005

Dear Great-Aunt Harriet,

What a conversation piece the door knocker is! We are especially pleased to have this memento of your travels in India and appreciate your effort in bringing it back.

Many thanks.

MEGALOPOLIS UNIVERSITY

3700 West Juniper Boulevard
Atlanta, Georgia 54321

Office of The Dean of Students   (123) 333-9999, Fax (123) 444-8888

November 15, 2005

Dear Roy:

Tom and I want to thank you for the many kindnesses you showed Mark when he visited your campus last weekend. He has returned full of enthusiasm for Handler College. Having been raised in the shadow of a large university, he found the close relationships of students and faculty at Handler particularly exciting.

You were right on target to arrange an interview with Dr. Strangelove of the Physics Department and to have a student take Mark to a soccer game. Seeing the well-equipped laboratories and the spirit of the athletes confirmed his belief that he has chosen the right school.

If you will be in our area in the coming months, do give us a call. We would enjoy having you come for dinner and an evening of catching up. Give Ellen our regards.

Cordially,

Della Kate Ayers

Dr. Roy L. DeCree
Office of the President
Handler College
Simpkins, North Carolina 25678

▢ Keeping in touch.

Personal letters are one of the best ways to maintain long-distance friendships. Write your news and observations with the reader in mind, recounting things that may be of particular interest. Responding to something in a previous letter or asking questions and inviting comment will stimulate a response that keeps the correspondence flowing.

> ✓ Informal Format, possibly handwritten

August 15, 2005

Dear Bill,

Your letter describing life in the big city arrived last week. I can see why you needed to leave our quiet little town behind! Cafes and clubs, museums and theater—it all seems to suit you so well. And I'm glad to hear that you are making new friends so easily.

It doesn't seem like a long time since you left, but now that I think about it, a lot has happened. We finished the little studio building out in the garden, and now I have a lovely place to paint, weave, and just get away from the hubbub. Cindy's goat won a blue ribbon at the county fair, and Jeff took up in-line skating. I never thought I'd be driving my kid into town just so he could find some pavement to skate on!

Our business is now a year old, and doing well enough that we may actually be able to take a vacation next year. In the meantime, the joys of home-based self-employment make up for the pressures of getting a new business off the ground.

Everyone here misses you, so do keep writing. When will you be back for a visit? Make sure to let us know, and we'll throw a party in your honor--if you can stand all the attention!

Love,

Sarah

▢ Travel.

When you travel to interesting places, writing to friends or relatives lets you share your experiences with them. Too often, however, letters describing a trip are not much more than an itinerary: "I went here and there—I saw this and that." Your reader would probably rather hear some anecdotes of your adventures, or your reaction to what you have seen. You needn't cover the whole trip, just those aspects you think would be of most interest to a particular reader. For example:

Greetings from Switzerland!

This country has certainly lived up to all the advance reports. The scenery is every bit as spectacular as it looks in the picture books—and the trains do run on time.

Switzerland is my candidate for the cleanest country in the world. Every house and yard is immaculate. Land is too valuable to let junk accumulate on it; it is all put to good use, for people or animals.

One of the most common uses is to grow vegetables and flowers. Every house has its vegetable garden; we even saw vegetables being grown between the tracks on a railroad siding! And every house where we have been guests had fresh flowers on the table, even though it's winter. Perhaps the gray weather at this time of year makes the addition of some bright colors a virtual necessity. Whatever the reason, I'm impressed by the year-round fresh-flower habit of the Swiss.

▯ To your children.

Over the centuries, parents have used letters to advise their children: study hard, resist temptations, make them proud, avoid bad companions, take care of their health—and write home! Mail from home is usually welcomed, but not if it turns out to be a lecture in longhand. Such letters are usually ineffective. For example, Lady Churchill wrote to her 15-year-old son:

Darling Winston,

I hope you will try and not smoke. If only you knew how foolish and silly you look doing it, you would give it up....

Letters from home can be one of the best ways to hold a family together over long distances; they do that job best when you use them to share your thoughts and show your affection. Be on the lookout for amusing incidents or local gossip to include in your letter.

May 30, 2005

Dear Mark,

Yesterday I bumped into your friend Tim Burr at the gas station. He and his brother Lum are already home from college, but they are getting ready to leave for their summer jobs. You will be green with envy when you hear what they will be doing: smoke jumping! They are excited at such a bold departure from their usual summer jobs at McDonald's, as you can imagine. But I must admit I don't envy their mother and father the summer of worry that lies ahead for them.

Jennie performed in her annual piano recital last week, and you will be impressed with how much she has learned since you heard her play at Christmas time. No more silly tunes like "Starlight Waltz" for her—she's now into Bach Minuets and Airs.

Dad hauled out the lawnmower last weekend for his first attack on the grass this year. It made me realize that summer will soon be here, and so will you.

Good luck with exams. Cookies will be on their way shortly to help you survive.

Love from the whole gang,

⬦ Sympathy.

For some, the most difficult letters to write are those expressing sympathy. If you are one of those, perhaps you feel awkward about communicating emotions to someone who has suffered the loss of a loved one; you hesitate to write, fearing that the words you choose will be clumsy or inadequate. But remember, many people feel such hesitation. As a result, the person experiencing grief may be cut off from much-needed support. Reaching out with a few carefully chosen words is a very human thing to do.

Your letter need not be long. If you are not a close friend or member of the family, a couple of sentences will suffice. Your personal note will mean more to the recipient than a purchased card.

A brief letter to someone who is not a close friend might be along the lines of the following examples. (Do write your message by hand.)

Letter 1:

The news of your loss has saddened us both.
We send you our sympathy at this difficult time.

Letter 2:

It was with sadness that I learned of your wife's death. Please accept my sincere condolences.

Letter 3:

While no word of mine can ease your loss, I want you to know that you are in my thoughts at this time of sorrow.

When you had a close relationship with the deceased, sharing your thoughts and feelings can be a comfort to the family. Anecdotes that reveal the person's character are welcomed as a way to keep alive the memory of the loved one.

Michael's death came as a tragic shock. Few seemed more full of life than he, making the loss all the more keenly felt by us all. Mike was one of the most mature young men I have known. He always knew the right thing to do to put everyone at ease, and could usually find something to laugh about—including his own mistakes.

This period of grieving Michael's death will be difficult for you. We miss him too, but he is very much alive in the memory of all who knew him. Our thoughts and prayers are with you.

When death comes in later years, your letter can mention the long, full life of the person. When an infant or child dies, your letter would usually acknowledge the untimely loss.

Letters of sympathy reflect the character and beliefs of the person writing them. Obviously, you should not use the occasion to try to convert the recipient to a particular point of view, but you should feel free to express yourself in religious terms if those are the words that come to you naturally. Divergence of religious beliefs is unimportant when the desire to console is sincere.

▯ Response to a sympathy letter.

A brief note is usually sent in response to expressions of sympathy. A few lines are all that is needed.

(1) *Thank you for being so thoughtful. Letters such as yours have meant a great deal to me at this time.*

(2) *Your memories of my father were a source of great joy to me. Thank you for sharing them with me.*

AS CONSUMER AND CITIZEN

You have the power to influence corporations and government officials. One of the best ways to exercise that influence is by writing letters.

Your letters will be most effective if they are directed to a specific individual. The reference librarian at your local library can probably help with names and addresses of corporate officers or elected officials.

▯ Complaint letter.

Consumer attitudes and satisfaction are carefully monitored by most companies. If you have cause for complaint—sloppy workmanship, unsatisfactory service, or objectionable advertising policies, for example—speak up about it.

If you think your complaint deserves a wide audience, you might want to send copies of your letter to appropriate agencies. The Food and Drug Administration, the Federal Trade Commission, and the Better Business Bureau respond to consumer complaints, and knowing they are hearing from you might ratchet up the interest of the offending company in rectifying a problem. Reserve this approach for important grievances, however.

Draw up an outline of your case before you start writing; facts and emotions often become tangled if you don't first sort them out. You may be boiling mad, but unless you make it clear to your reader *why* you are angry, you may be treated as "just another crank." Putting the reader on the defensive will not further your cause. Express your complaint or anger responsibly, assuming that the reader is intelligent and wants to hear your views.

✓ Simplified Letter Format
✓ Complaint Letter

November 30, 2005

Morgan County District Court
837 East Fourth Avenue
Wilsonville, IN 45678

SUMMONS D29783584

I do not deny that I was driving above the speed limit on River Road on November 3, 2005. I accept the fact that I needed a reprimand. I would like, however, to request that the court consider lowering the amount of my bail.

I believe that I was driving safely, given the road and traffic conditions, at ten miles per hour above the posted speed limit. The driver of the car ahead of me apparently thought so, too, as he was traveling even faster than I was (and didn't get ticketed!). Under the circumstances, I find the bail of $150 to be excessive. Please reconsider whether the punishment fits the crime.

Thank you.

Cliff Hangar

Cliff Hangar
598 Gerber Street, Apt. 3
Williamsville, IN 45921

CHASTITY LAWES / 987 Overlook Lane, Madison, New Jersey 07652 (210) 679-0985

February 6, 2005

Customer Relations
Patriot's Bank
524 Lakeside Drive
Madison, NJ 07654

STATUS OF ACCOUNT NO. XXXXXX

I would like to clear up a problem that began when I opened a checking account at Patriot's Bank last month. Your employee failed to give me a New Customer Information brochure at that time. Lacking the critical information that is in the brochure, I now find myself owing several hundred dollars without ever having overdrawn my account. Here's how the problem developed.

When I opened the account, I left with temporary checks in hand, a significant balance in my account, and a general sense of confidence that I knew how to operate a checking account. A couple of weeks later, the "bounced check" notices began to arrive. Soon afterward, a notice from Patriot's informed me that a two-week hold had been placed on my initial deposit. This is the first I was told that such a long hold would be instituted.

But that was just the beginning of the trouble. I had written several checks before receiving the notice of the two-week hold. Consequently, without my knowledge, I was placed in a "bad customer" category that required long holds on all of my deposits. Despite adequate deposits on my part, even more checks bounced. One of those checks was for my vehicle registration.

I now owe Patriot's, several businesses, and the Department of Motor Vehicles a total of $385 in "bounced check" fees. I am afraid to make deposits or write checks, because I have no idea what new policy, of which I have never been informed, will apply.

Please attend to this matter immediately. Since I am innocent of any wrongdoing, I believe that Patriot's should reimburse me for all overdraft fees and remove any negative judgments from my account.

I look forward to hearing from you soon, informing me that my account has been restored to normal status, and that I may once again write checks with peace of mind.

Chastity Lawes

CHASTITY LAWES

P.S. Please send me a New Customer Information brochure.

Ida Claire
Post Office Box 007
Grover, CA 90000

June 14, 2005

Mr. Forrest Greene, President
Cleanmore Manufacturing Company
345 Industrial Parkway
Cleveland, Ohio 44000

Dear Mr. Greene:

Subject: Model 35-X Cleanmore Washer, purchased on January 10, 2005

As president of Cleanmore, you are undoubtedly interested in the consumer's view of your products and service. I have been a Cleanmore buyer for more than 20 years and have always found your appliances to perform satisfactorily; in fact, I never had to think about them. That is why my problems with the washer I recently purchased have been such an unpleasant surprise.

One month after I purchased the washer, it started overflowing, creating a major cleanup problem in the kitchen. Since it was well within the three-month guarantee period, I requested repairs. The service representative who arrived said she would have to return with a replacement part for the control panel; it was two weeks before she returned. The machine operated satisfactorily for one month and then started overflowing again. This time the service department took three weeks to respond; when the service rep arrived, he lacked the necessary part. Further delays pushed his return past the warranty period.

You can imagine my shock when I received a bill for $198 for this "service." My protests that the service department delays were the reason the machine was no longer under warranty were politely rejected. At least they were polite. But that doesn't diminish my anger over such unfair treatment.

I believe in going right to the top when I have a problem. I am therefore writing to ask for your help in correcting what surely must be an improper interpretation of your warranty. I look forward to hearing from you.

Sincerely,

Ida Claire

Ida Claire
Enclosure

✎ Letter to government representative.

Government representatives, including the President, are influenced by the *quantity* of mail they receive regarding specific bills or legislative issues. They tally the "Yeas" and "Nays" to gauge public sentiment.

But elected officials are also interested in the *quality* of the letters they receive. Letters that are clearly individually written may be given special attention, especially if they follow these guidelines.

- Keep your letter short; no more than one page, if possible.
- Use legible handwriting or type the letter. If it is typed, add a short, handwritten postscript to give the letter a personal touch.
- Spell the representative's name correctly.
- If appropriate, identify pending legislation by name and bill number.
- Briefly explain the reasons behind your position—how a bill might create problems or alleviate them.
- Indicate the action you want the legislator to take.
- Be helpful rather than threatening; hostility is counter-productive.
- Stick to one issue. It's tempting to rattle off a whole laundry list of problems you would like to have solved, but your letter will be more effective if you limit yourself to one issue at a time.
- Include your return address.

WHITEHALL UNIVERSITY

22 University Way, Whitehall, Pennsylvania 26789
(209) 543-0987, Fax (209) 777-9090

October 8, 2005

Senator Hugh N. Krye
United States Senate
Washington, D. C. 20510

Dear Senator Krye:

I am writing to express my alarm about the University Research Funding Bill, S369, which is presently being debated in the Senate. If passed, this bill would drastically curtail funding for basic research in our universities. While proponents of the bill argue that "applied" and "relevant" research will still be funded, my experience says that their view is dangerously narrow.

As a professor of physics at Whitehall University for the past twenty years, I have sponsored dozens of graduate students in research projects ranging from the highly theoretical to the obviously applicable. The irony of such terms is that, in the final analysis, practical applications have arisen from "theoretical" research just as often as from "applied" research.

Limiting funding to projects of known value is similar to allowing gold prospectors to explore only areas with known ore-bearing potential; they will probably find gold, but they are not likely to make new discoveries.

Recent studies have shown that the economic return from basic research is higher in the United States than among other industrialized nations. This may well be a result of the activities and accomplishments of our graduate students. The fundamental research these students conduct is now the kind that is coming under fire by congressional critics who want to limit government support to "practical" applications.

I urge you, for the health of both our universities and the nation, to vote against S369.

Very truly yours,

Mason Jarrs

Dr. Mason Jarrs

Representatives in government also like to hear from you when you approve of their position or actions. If you want to encourage them to continue in a certain direction, let them know you appreciated their vote. A thank-you, in the sea of demands and complaints, is like a breath of fresh air.

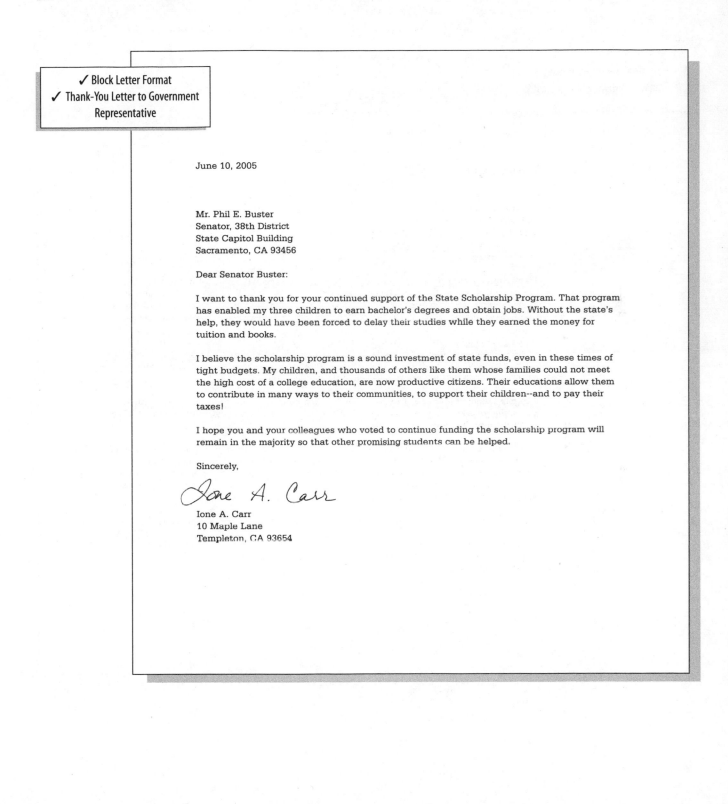

✓ Block Letter Format
✓ Thank-You Letter to Government
Representative

June 10, 2005

Mr. Phil E. Buster
Senator, 38th District
State Capitol Building
Sacramento, CA 93456

Dear Senator Buster:

I want to thank you for your continued support of the State Scholarship Program. That program has enabled my three children to earn bachelor's degrees and obtain jobs. Without the state's help, they would have been forced to delay their studies while they earned the money for tuition and books.

I believe the scholarship program is a sound investment of state funds, even in these times of tight budgets. My children, and thousands of others like them whose families could not meet the high cost of a college education, are now productive citizens. Their educations allow them to contribute in many ways to their communities, to support their children--and to pay their taxes!

I hope you and your colleagues who voted to continue funding the scholarship program will remain in the majority so that other promising students can be helped.

Sincerely,

Ione A. Carr

Ione A. Carr
10 Maple Lane
Templeton, CA 93654

✐ Soliciting funds.

Organizations and schools often take to the mails to raise money for their continued existence. If you are called upon to write such a letter, make it as convincing and interesting as you can. You have a lot of competition in the mailbox, so it takes a careful choice of words—and maybe even a sense of humor—to make your letter stand out.

✓ Modified Block Format
✓ Letter Soliciting Funds

IVY LEAGUE
987 Mountain Road
Jamestown, AL 39090

May 1, 2005

Dear Classmate:

Lie still now, and let me drop some water on your forehead.

At least that may feel like what I'm doing with my annual reminder of the need to support Ivy College. But it frequently requires repetition to produce action--and action may be appropriate with regard to disposition of your worldly goods.

If you haven't reviewed your will for a number of years, you might be surprised to see how quickly it has become outdated. Or, if you have never taken the time to write your will, there's no better time than right now, while your faculties are still in reasonably good working order.

In any event, may I urge you to consider including Ivy in your planning? Did you realize that you can receive both tax benefits and income during your lifetime if you establish an Ivy Donor Trust? It's a straightforward procedure, as the enclosed brochure indicates. In these times when we are looking for value received for our contributions, the quality education that Ivy continues to offer its students looks like more and more of a bargain.

We have now been associated with Ivy College for one-third of its 90 years. The investment made in our education has continued to provide us with a variety of dividends over those years. Remembering Ivy in our estate planning will help assure that others will have a similar opportunity.

Best regards,

Ivy League

Ivy League

Enclosure

The following letter set some kind of record for political fund-raising. It was signed by eight women in the small community where I live and went to a mailing list of hundreds, not thousands. But where a response rate of 2% is considered satisfactory for a direct solicitation, this letter had more than a 40% response. We achieved our financial goal several times over.

✓ Block Letter Format
✓ Letter Soliciting Funds

November 6, 2007

Dear Friend:

How about a fundraiser where we don't ask you to:

- buy or sell raffle tickets

- bake cookies

- knock on doors

- make phone calls

- run a 10K race

- make a quilt

- serve on a committee

- clean up afterward

In this community, where we are often asked to donate our time and energy to raise money for worthy causes, we thought the direct approach would be a refreshing change. So we're skipping the time-and-energy part and just asking for your money!

The worthy cause in this case is the candidacy of Warren Pease for U.S. Senate. Seldom do we have the chance to support a politician we can believe in, so the possibility of having someone with the integrity and vision of Mr. Pease representing us in the Senate is exciting. The enclosed flyer indicates some of the reasons for our enthusiasm.

The Pease campaign hopes to have 1,000 people each raise $1,000. That's an ambitious figure for our small community, but doing it would give these all-important early days of the campaign a boost.

If you agree, please make your check to "Warren Pease for U.S. Senate" and mail it to us in the enclosed envelope. We'll tally the proceeds and forward the checks to the Pease campaign.

Thank you!

Appendixes

Appendix A: Word Choices 152

       Strong Verbs

       Expressions to Avoid

Appendix B:
Postal Service Abbreviations. . . . 156

       Two-Letter State and

         Province Abbreviations

       Street Address Abbreviations

       Business Word Abbreviations

Appendix C: Forms of Address. . 161

Appendix D: Test Yourself 168

       Grammar and Usage

       Punctuation and Capitalization

       Style

       Spelling

Resources for
the Letter Writer. 182

Appendix A: Word Choices

Strong Verbs

Invigorate your writing by using strong verbs, such as the following.

accelerate	distribute	persuade
allocate	draft	prepare
analyze	eliminate	prioritize
approve	encourage	publicize
arbitrate	enlist	purchase
arrange	enlarge	recommend
assemble	evaluate	remodel
assign	examine	reorganize
build	expand	repair
calculate	explain	research
clarify	formulate	resolve
collaborate	generate	retrieve
collect	illustrate	revitalize
compile	improve	schedule
complete	increase	sell
consolidate	influence	shape
contract	initiate	simplify
convince	inspect	stabilize
coordinate	interview	streamline
create	investigate	survey
customize	invigorate	systematize
delegate	lecture	train
deliver	manage	trim
demonstrate	monitor	unravel
design	motivate	upgrade
diagnose	negotiate	widen
direct	operate	write

EXPRESSIONS TO AVOID

The words and phrases in the left-hand column are stilted or wordy. Delete them or rewrite using a suggested alternative.

Hackneyed Expression	Alternative
according to our records	we find
acknowledge receipt of	thank you for
afford an opportunity	allow, permit
along the lines of	like
as regards	regarding, concerning
at an early (a later) date	soon (later)
attached please find	I am attaching, I enclose
at the present time (writing)	now
at your earliest convenience	soon, as soon as possible
awaiting your instructions (reply)	please let us know, please reply
beg to state (differ, advise)	(delete)
bring to your attention	remind you
by means of	by
call your attention to	please note
deem	consider, think
despite the fact that	although
do not hesitate to	please
due to the fact that	because
duly	(delete)
enclosed please find	I enclose
feel free to call (write)	please call (write)
for the purpose of	for
for the reason that	because, since
give an answer	answer
give this matter your attention	attend to
have before me	received
in accordance with	as
in answer to	you asked
inasmuch as	since
in due course	soon
in order that	so that
in receipt of	received
in terms of	in
in the amount of	for
in the case of	(rewrite)
in the event that	if
in the near future	soon

Hackneyed Expression	Alternative
in the neighborhood of	about
in this connection	about this
I remain	(delete)
is indicative of	indicates
is in need of	needs
kindly	please
make inquiry regarding	inquire
May we have the pleasure of a reply?	May we hear from you?
meet with approval	approve
my personal opinion	my opinion
not in a position to	unable to
on behalf of	for
on the grounds that	because
our Ms. Wilson	Ms. Wilson
per	as
permit me to say	(delete)
please be advised that	(delete)
please do not hesitate to call	please call
prepared to offer	able to offer
present writer	I
prior to	before
pursuant to	following
referring to yours of May 9	your May 9 letter
regret to advise (inform)	unfortunately (*or* rewrite)
same	(rewrite)
subsequent to	after
take the liberty of	(delete)
take pleasure in	are happy to
take this opportunity	(delete)
under separate cover	by (FedEx, first class mail), separately
undersigned	I
until such time as	until
with all due regard	(delete)
with a view to	to
without further delay	now, immediately
with reference (regard, respect) to	about
with the result that	so that
would appreciate your informing (advising) us	please let us know

Appendix B: Postal Service Abbreviations

TWO-LETTER STATE ABBREVIATIONS

AL	Alabama	MT	Montana
AK	Alaska	NE	Nebraska
AZ	Arizona	NV	Nevada
AR	Arkansas	NH	New Hampshire
CA	California	NJ	New Jersey
CZ	Canal Zone	NM	New Mexico
CO	Colorado	NY	New York
CT	Connecticut	NC	North Carolina
DE	Delaware	ND	North Dakota
DC	District of Columbia	OH	Ohio
FL	Florida	OK	Oklahoma
GA	Georgia	OR	Oregon
GU	Guam	PA	Pennsylvania
HI	Hawaii	PR	Puerto Rico
ID	Idaho	RI	Rhode Island
IL	Illinois	SC	South Carolina
IN	Indiana	SD	South Dakota
IA	Iowa	TN	Tennessee
KS	Kansas	TX	Texas
KY	Kentucky	UT	Utah
LA	Louisiana	VT	Vermont
ME	Maine	VA	Virginia
MD	Maryland	VI	Virgin Islands
MA	Massachusetts	WA	Washington
MI	Michigan	WV	West Virginia
MN	Minnesota	WI	Wisconsin
MS	Mississippi	WY	Wyoming
MO	Missouri		

TWO-LETTER CANADIAN PROVINCE ABBREVIATIONS

AB	Alberta	NS	Nova Scotia
BC	British Columbia	ON	Ontario
LB	Labrador	PE	Prince Edward Island
MB	Manitoba	PQ	Quebec
NF	Newfoundland	SK	Saskatchewan
NT	Northwest Territories		

STREET ADDRESS ABBREVIATIONS
(recommended by the U.S. Postal Service)

Street Name	*USPS Abbreviation*	*Street Name*	*USPS Abbreviation*
ANNEX	ANX	GROVE	GRV
APARTMENT	APT	HARBOR	HBR
AVENUE	AVE	HEIGHTS	HTS
BEACH	BCH	HILL(S)	HL(S)
BOULEVARD	BLVD	HOLLOW	HOLW
BRANCH	BR	HIGHWAY	HWY
BRIDGE	BRG	INTERSTATE	INTSTE
BROOK	BRK	ISLAND	IS
BYPASS	BYP	JUNCTION	JCT
CANYON	CYN	KEY	KY
CAUSEWAY	CSWY	KNOLLS	KNLS
CENTER	CTR	LAKE	LK
CIRCLE	CIR	LANDING	LNDG
CORNER(S)	COR(S)	LANE	LN
COURT	CT	MANOR	MNR
CRESCENT	CRES	MEADOWS	MDWS
CREEK	CK	MISSION	MSN
CROSSING	XING	MOUNT(AIN)	MT(N)
DRIVE	DR	PARK	PARK
ESTATE	EST	PARKWAY	PKY
EXPRESSWAY	EXPY	PASS	PASS
EXTENSION	EXT	PIKE	PIKE
FALLS	FLS	PINES	PNES
FERRY	FRY	PLACE	PL
FOREST	FRST	PLAIN(S)	PLN(S)
FORGE	FRG	PLAZA	PLZ
GARDENS	GDNS	POINT	PT
GATEWAY	GTWY	PORT	PRT
GLEN	GLN	PRAIRIE	PR

RANCH	RNCH	TERRACE	TER
RAPIDS	RPDS	TRAIL	TRL
ROAD	RD	TURNPIKE	TPKE
RIDGE	RDG	VALLEY	VLY
RIVER	RIV	UNION	UN
SHOAL	SHL	VIADUCT	VIA
SHORE(S)	SHR(S)	VIEW	VW
SPRING(S)	SPG(S)	VILLAGE	VLG
SQUARE	SQ	VISTA	VIS
STREET	ST	WALK	WALK
STATION	STA	WAY	WAY
STREAM	STRM	WELLS	WLS
SUMMIT	SMT		

BUSINESS WORD ABBREVIATIONS
(recommended by the U.S. Postal Service)

Business Word	*USPS Abbreviation*	*Business Word*	*USPS Abbreviation*
ACADEMY	ACDMY	COMPANY	CO
ADMINIS-TRATION	ADMN	COMPTROLLER	COMPTLR
AGENCY	AGCY	COMPUTER	CMPTR
AMERICA	AMER	CONDOMINIUM	CONDO
AMERICAN	AMERCN	CONFERENCE	CNFRNC
ASSOCIATE	ASSOC	CONGRESS	CNGRS
ASSOCIATION	ASSN	CONGRESSIONAL	CNGRSNL
ATLANTIC	ATL	CONGRESSMAN	CONGRSMN
ATTENTION	ATTN	CONGRESSWOMAN	CONGRSWMN
ATTORNEY	ATTY	CONSUMER	CONSMR
BANK	BK	CORPORAL	CORPL
BANKING	BNKNG	CORPORATION	CORP
BROKER	BRKR	COUNCIL	CNCL
BUREAU	BUR	DEPARTMENT	DEPT
BUSINESS	BUS	DIRECTOR	DIR
CHAIR	CHR	DISTRIBUTING	DISTRG
CHAIRMAN	CHRMN	EASTERN	ESTRN
CHAIRWOMAN	CHRWMN	ELECTRONIC	ELECT
COLLEGE	COLG	ELEMENTARY	ELEM
COLONEL	COL	EMBASSY	EMBSSY
COMMANDER	CMDR	EMPLOYMENT	EMPLMNT
COMMERCE	COMMRCE	ENGINEER	ENGR
COMMERCIAL	COMRCL	ENGINEERING	ENGRG
COMMISSION	COMM	ENVIRONMENT	ENVIR
COMMITTEE	CMMTE	ENVIRONMENTAL	ENVIRON
COMMON-WEALTH	CMNWLTH	ESTABLISHMENT	ESTAB
COMMUNI-CATION	COMMCTN	EXTENSION	EXT

FEDERAL	FED	MUNICIPAL	MNCPL
FEDERATED	FDRTD	MUTUAL	MUTL
FEDERATION	FEDRN	NATIONAL	NATL
FIDELITY	FIDLTY	NORTHERN	NTHRN
FINANCIAL	FNCL	NORTHWESTERN	NWN
FORCE	FRC	OFFICE	OFC
FOREMAN	FORMN	ORGANIZATION	ORGN
FOUNDATION	FNDTN	PACIFIC	PAC
GENERAL	GEN	PAYABLE	PAYABL
GOVERNMENT	GOVT	PERSONNEL	PRSNNL
GROUP	GRP	PLANNING	PLAN
HEADQUARTERS	HDQTRS	PROGRAM	PRGM
HONORABLE	HON	PURCHASER	PURCHR
HOTEL	HTL	RAILWAY	RLWY
INCORPORATED	INC	REALTY	RLTY
INDUSTRIAL	IND	RECEIVABLE	RCVBL
INFORMATION	INFO	REFINING	RFNG
INSTITUTE	INST	REGION	REGN
INSURANCE	INS	SAVINGS	SVNGS
INTERNATIONAL	INTRNTL	SECRETARY	SECY
LABORATORY	LAB	SENATOR	SEN
LIBRARY	LBRY	SERVICE	SVC
LIEUTENANT	LT	SUPERINTENDENT	SUPT
LIMITED	LTD	SUPERVISOR	SUPVSR
MANAGEMENT	MGMT	SUPPLY	SUPL
MANAGER	MGR	SYSTEM	SYST
MANUFAC-TURING	MFG	TECHNICAL	TECHL
MARKET	MKT	TECHNOLOGY	TECHLGY
MERCHANDISE	MDSE	TERMINAL	TRML
MIDDLE	MID	TRAINING	TRAIN
MIDTOWN	MDTWN	TREASURER	TRES
MIDWEST	MDWST	WESTERN	WSTRN
MINISTRY	MNSTRY	WORLD	WLD
MONUMENT	MNMT		

Appendix C: Forms of Address

Addressee	Address on Letter and Envelope	Salutation and Complimentary Close
GOVERNMENT		

The President	The President
	The White House
	Washington, DC 20500
		Dear Mr. President:
		Dear Madam President:
		  Respectfully, *or*
		  Most respectfully,

Wife of the President	Mrs. (surname)
	The White House
	Washington, DC 20500
		Dear Mrs. (surname):
		  Very truly yours, *or*
		  Sincerely yours,

The Vice President	The Vice President
	United States Senate
	Washington, DC 20510
	or
	The Honorable (full name)
	Vice President of the United States
	Washington, DC 20501
		Dear Mr. Vice President:
		Dear Madam Vice President:
		  Very truly yours, *or*
		  Sincerely yours,

The Chief Justice	The Chief Justice of the United States
	The Supreme Court of the United States
	Washington, DC 20543
		Dear Mr. Chief Justice:
		Dear Madam Chief Justice:
		  Very truly yours, *or*
		  Sincerely yours,

Associate Justice	Mr. Justice (surname)
	Madam Justice (surname)
	The Supreme Court of the United States
	Washington, DC 20543
		Dear Mr. Justice:
		Dear Madam Justice:
		  Very truly yours, *or*
		  Sincerely yours,

United States Senator	Honorable (full name)
	United States Senate
	Washington, DC 20515
	or
	Honorable (full name)
	United States Senator
	(local address)
		Dear Senator (surname):
		  Very truly yours, *or*
		  Sincerely yours,

United States Representative	Honorable (full name) House of Representatives Washington, DC 20515 *or* Honorable (full name) Member, United States House of Representatives (local address)	Dear (Mr., Mrs., Ms.) (surname): Very truly yours, *or* Sincerely yours,
Cabinet Members	Honorable (full name) Secretary of (name of department) Washington, DC (ZIP)	Dear Mr. Secretary: Dear Madam Secretary: Very truly yours, *or* Sincerely yours,
Ambassador, U.S.	Honorable (full name) The American Ambassador American Embassy (Street) (City) (COUNTRY)	Dear Mr. Ambassador: Dear Madam Ambassador: Very truly yours, *or* Sincerely yours,
Ambassador, Foreign	His (Her) Excellency (full name) Ambassador of (country) (street) (city), (state) (ZIP)	Excellency: *or* Dear Mr. (Mrs., Ms.) Ambassador: Very truly yours,
Governor	Honorable (full name) Governor of (state) State Capitol (city), (state) (ZIP)	Dear Governor (surname): Very truly yours, *or* Sincerely yours,
State Senator, Representative, Assemblyperson	Honorable (full name) (office address)	Dear (Mr., Mrs., Ms.) (surname) Very truly yours, *or* Sincerely yours,
Mayor	Honorable (full name) Mayor of (name of city) City Hall (city), (state) (ZIP)	Dear Mayor (surname): *or* Dear (Mr., Mrs., Ms.) (surname) Very truly yours, *or* Sincerely yours,
Judge	Honorable (full name) (name of court) (local address)	Dear Judge (surname): Very truly yours, *or* Sincerely yours,

FOREIGN HEADS OF STATE

Premier	His (Her) Excellency (full name) Premier of (country) (street) (city) (COUNTRY)	Dear Mr. (Mrs., Ms.) Premier: Very truly yours,

| President of a Republic | His (Her) Excellency (full name)
President of (country)
(street)
(city)
(COUNTRY) | Excellency:
Dear Mr. (Madam) President:
  Very truly yours, |
| Prime Minister | His (Her) Excellency (full name)
(street)
(city)
(COUNTRY) | Excellency:
Dear Mr. (Mrs., Ms.) Prime Minister:
  Very truly yours, |

CHURCH/SYNAGOGUE

Protestant

Episcopal Clergy	The Right Reverend (full name)
	Bishop of (name)
	(local address)
	or
	The Very Reverend (full name)
	Dean of (name)
	(local address)
		Dear Bishop (surname):
		  Very truly yours, *or*
		  Sincerely yours,
		
		Dear Dean (surname):
		  Very truly yours, *or*
		  Sincerely yours,

Clergy with Doctoral Degree	The Reverend (full name), D. D.
	(local address)
		Dear Dr. (surname): *or*
		Dear Reverend (surname):
		  Very truly yours, *or*
		  Sincerely yours,

Clergy without Doctoral Degree	The Reverend (full name)
	(local address)
		Dear Reverend (surname): *or*
		Dear (Mr., Mrs., Ms.) (surname):
		  Very truly yours, *or*
		  Sincerely yours,

Catholic

| The Pope | His Holiness, the Pope *or*
His Holiness Pope (name)
Vatican City
00187 Rome
ITALY | Your Holiness, *or*
Most Holy Father,
  Your Holiness' most humble servant, |
| Cardinal | His Eminence (given name)
Cardinal (surname)
Archbishop of (diocese)
(local address) | Your Eminence: (formal) *or*
Dear Cardinal (surname): (less formal)
  Very truly yours, *or*
  Sincerely yours, |

Bishop or Archbishop	The Most Reverend (full name) Bishop of (diocese) *or* Archbishop of (diocese) (local address)	Your Excellency: (formal) *or* Dear Archbishop (surname): (less formal) Very truly yours, *or* Sincerely yours,
Other Catholic Clergy	The Right Reverend Monsignor (full name) (local address)	Right Reverend Monsignor: (formal) Dear Monsignor (surname): (less formal) Very truly yours, *or* Sincerely,
	The Reverend (full name and initials of order, if used) (local address)	Reverend Sir: (formal) Dear Father (surname): (less formal) Very truly yours, *or* Sincerely,
	Mother (full name and initials of order, if used) (local address)	Dear Mother (full name): Very truly yours, *or* Sincerely,
	Sister (full name and initials of order, if used) (local address)	Dear Sister (full name): Very truly yours, *or* Sincerely,

Jewish

With Scholastic Degree	Rabbi (full name), D.D., LL.D. (local address)	Dear Rabbi (surname): *or* Dear Dr. (surname): Very truly yours, *or* Sincerely yours,
Without Scholastic Degree	Rabbi (full name) (local address)	Dear Rabbi (surname): Very truly yours, *or* Sincerely yours,

SCHOOLS

President of a College or University	Dr. (full name) President, (name of institution) (local address)	Dear Dr. (surname): Very truly yours, *or* Sincerely yours,
Dean	Dean (full name) School of (name) (name of institution) (local address)	Dear Dean (surname) Very truly yours, *or* Sincerely yours,
Professor	Professor (full name) Department of (name) (name of institution) (local address)	Dear Professor (surname) Very truly yours, *or* Sincerely yours,

MILITARY

For Any Branch of Service:

(Full or abbreviated rank) (full name), (abbreviation of branch of service: USA, USAF, USCG, USMC, or USN) (military address) (ZIP)	Dear (full rank) (surname): Very truly yours, *or* Sincerely yours,

U.S. Army, Air Force, and Marine Corps Personnel

General	General Thomas Cook U.S. Marine Corps (post office address of organization and station)	Dear General Cook: Very truly yours, *or* Sincerely yours,
Major General	Major General Sarah Forbes U.S. Air Force (post office address of organization and station)	Dear General Forbes: Very truly yours, *or* Sincerely yours,
Lieutenant Colonel	Lieutenant Colonel James Hartley, U.S. Army (post office address of organization and station)	Dear Colonel Hartley: Very truly yours, *or* Sincerely yours,
Captain	Captain Mary Miller, U.S. Air Force (post office address of organization and station)	Dear Captain Miller: Very truly yours, *or* Sincerely yours,
Second Lieutenant	Second Lieutenant Wayne Jonas, U.S. Marine Corps (post office address of organization and station)	Dear Lieutenant Jonas: Very truly yours, *or* Sincerely yours,
Warrant Officer	Warrant Officer Norman Abbott, U.S. Army (post office address of organization and station)	Dear Mr. Abbott: Very truly yours, *or* Sincerely yours,
Sergeant Major	Sergeant Major Ann Owens, U.S. Marine Corps (post office address of organization and station)	Dear Sergeant Major Owens: Very truly yours, *or* Sincerely yours,
Master Sergeant	Master Sergeant Adam Bates, U.S. Air Force (post office address of organization and station)	Dear Sergeant Bates: Very truly yours, *or* Sincerely yours,

Corporal	Corporal Kate Merritt, U.S. Army (post office address of organization and station)	Dear Corporal Merritt: Very truly yours, *or* Sincerely yours,
Private First Class or Private	(Rank) Samuel Tarcher, U.S Marine Corps. (post office address of organization and station)	Dear Private Tarcher: Very truly yours, *or* Sincerely yours,
Airman First Class, Airman, or Basic Airman	(Rank) Leslie Brandt, U.S. Air Force (post office address of organization and station)	Dear Airman Brandt: Very truly yours, *or* Sincerely yours,

Navy personnel

Admiral	Admiral Alice Wong, U.S. Navy (post office address of organization and station)	Dear Admiral Wong: Very truly yours, *or* Sincerely yours,
Rear Admiral	Rear Admiral Ellis Watts, U.S. Navy (post office address of organization and station)	Dear Admiral Watts: Very truly yours, *or* Sincerely yours,
Captain	Captain Susan Schmidt, U.S. Navy (post office address of organization and station)	Dear Captain Schmidt: Very truly yours, *or* Sincerely yours,
Lieutenant Commander	Lieutenant Commander Roy Dennis, U.S. Navy (post office address of organization and station)	Dear Commander Dennis: Very truly yours, *or* Sincerely yours,
Lieutenant	Lieutenant Barbara Sims, U.S. Navy (post office address of organization and station)	Dear Ms. Sims: Very truly yours, *or* Sincerely yours,
Ensign	Ensign Orville Peters, U.S. Navy (post office address of organization and station)	Dear Mr. Peters: Very truly yours, *or* Sincerely yours,
Warrant Officer (all grades)	Warrant Officer Doris Babcock, U.S. Navy (post office address of organization and station)	Dear Ms. Babcock: Very truly yours, *or* Sincerely yours,
Enlisted Personnel (all grades)	(Rank) (full name), U.S. Navy (post office address of organization and station)	Dear (Mr., Ms.) (surname): Very truly yours, *or* Sincerely yours,

Retired Military Personnel

All	(Rank) (full name), (abbreviation of service designation), Retired (local address)	Dear (rank) (surname): Very truly yours, *or* Sincerely yours,
Example:	Brigadier General Eric Olsen, U.S. Army, Retired 3847 Victory Boulevard Sun City, AZ 83111	Dear General Olsen: Very truly yours, *or* Sincerely yours,

Appendix D: Test Yourself

Do your language skills need polishing? Take the quizzes on the following pages to test your grasp of the fundamentals of grammar, punctuation, style, and spelling. Errors suggest areas where review would be appropriate.

Correct answers appear on the page facing each quiz. Cover the answers if you tend to look at them before completing the quiz. Refer to *Write Right!* or other books listed in "Resources for the Letter Writer" for help with any aspects of language you need to brush up.

Grammar and Usage:

Choose the correct word or words in parentheses in the following sentences.

1. Only one in four (use, uses) our products.
2. The number of books published (has, have) grown steadily over the past decade.
3. The contract was awarded to my partner and (I, me, myself).
4. My partner and (I, me, myself) are planning to move to a larger office.
5. Between you and (I, me), the move is long overdue.
6. You drive more carefully than (I, me).
7. I (can, cannot) see hardly any reason for his behavior.
8. Answer (whoever, whomever) asks for information.
9. To (who, whom) shall I report?
10. The one (who, whom) we all admire is Josephine.
11. The media (is, are) often criticized.
12. The criteria for admission (is, are) as follows.
13. A selection of patterns (are, is) available.
14. The title and abstract of the report (is, are) printed on the first page.
15. A number of stock market indicators (was, were) favorable.
16. The number of applicants (is, are) decreasing.
17. Neither of the examples (was, were) correct.
18. Either personal checks or major credit cards (is, are) accepted for payment.
19. The company notified (its, it's, their) employees.
20. When the jury returned (its, it's, their) verdict, everyone was stunned.
21. *An acquaintance is a person (who, whom) we know well enough to borrow from, but not well enough to lend to.* —Ambrose Bierce

Grammar and Usage Corrected Version:

1. Only one in four uses our products.

2. The number of books published has grown steadily over the past decade.

3. The contract was awarded to my partner and me.

4. My partner and I are planning to move to a larger office.

5. Between you and me, the move is long overdue.

6. You drive more carefully than I.

7. I can see hardly any reason for his behavior (*or* I cannot see any reason for his behavior).

8. Answer whoever asks for information.

9. To whom shall I report?

10. The one whom we all admire is Josephine.

11. The media are often criticized.

12. The criteria for admission are as follows.

13. A selection of patterns is available.

14. The title and abstract of the report are printed on the first page.

15. A number of stock market indicators were favorable.

16. The number of applicants is decreasing.

17. Neither of the examples was correct.

18. Either personal checks or major credit cards are accepted for payment.

19. The company notified its employees.

20. When the jury returned its verdict, everyone was stunned.

21. *An acquaintance is a person whom we know well enough to borrow from, but not well enough to lend to.* —Ambrose Bierce

22. *People (who, whom) say they sleep like a baby usually don't have one.* —Leo J. Burke

23. The program is not going (nowhere, anywhere).

24. The move will not (affect, effect) our Customer Service Department.

25. The (affect, effect) will be noticed in our speed of response.

26. (Its, It's) important that we speed up response time.

27. Her work (complemented, complimented) the efforts of her staff.

28. He sought (council, counsel) from his attorney.

29. John ate (fewer, less) hot dogs than Mary.

30. The company will need new (stationary, stationery).

31. Earnings of high-tech companies (comprise, constitute) only six percent of GNP.

32. The treasurer (dispersed, disbursed) the remaining funds.

33. We need to (home, hone) in on our objective.

34. The medic (stanched, staunched) the flow of blood.

35. The new prime minister inherited the (reigns, reins) of government at a time of turmoil; her (reign, rein) may be cut short.

36. The payment must include both (principle, principal) and interest.

37. We visited the (Capital, Capitol) building.

38. The supervisor (complemented, complimented) the crew on the quality of their work.

39. They moved (farther, further) from town.

40. The (phenomena, phenomenon) is widespread.

41. Three-fourths of the ballots (has, have) been counted.

42. The author wrote the (foreword, forward, foreward) of the book.

43. The culprits received their just (deserts, desserts).

44. Her writing style is different (from, than) mine.

45. I (would of, would have) been on time, but I had a flat tire.

46. (Whose, Who's) hat is this?

47. We (use to, used to) offer discounts to full-time employees.

48. They will consider the proposal (farther, further).

49. One-half of the money (is, are) missing.

50. (Fewer, less) than five people attended.

22. *People who say they sleep like a baby usually don't have one.* —Leo J. Burke

23. The program is not going anywhere (*or* The program is going nowhere).

24. The move will not affect our Customer Service Department.

25. The effect will be noticed in our speed of response.

26. It's important that we speed up response time.

27. Her work complemented the efforts of her staff.

28. He sought counsel from his attorney.

29. John ate fewer hot dogs than Mary.

30. The company will need new stationery.

31. Earnings of high-tech companies constitute only six percent of GNP.

32. The treasurer disbursed the remaining funds.

33. We need to home in on our objective.

34. The medic stanched the flow of blood.

35. The new prime minister inherited the reins of government at a time of turmoil; her reign may be cut short.

36. The payment must include both principal and interest.

37. We visited the Capitol building.

38. The supervisor complimented the crew on the quality of their work.

39. They moved farther from town.

40. The phenomenon is widespread.

41. Three-fourths of the ballots have been counted.

42. The author wrote the foreword of the book.

43. The culprits received their just desserts.

44. Her writing style is different from mine.

45. I would have been on time, but I had a flat tire.

46. Whose hat is this?

47. We used to offer discounts to full-time employees.

48. They will consider the proposal further.

49. One-half of the money is missing.

50. Fewer than five people attended.

Punctuation and Capitalization:

Capitalize and punctuate the following sentences, where needed. **Warning**: *Some of the sentences are correct, as is.*

51. She is taking a months vacation.

52. The average urban voter does not appear in the polls.

53. A young energetic student could handle the assignment.

54. On Friday I phoned his office and spoke with him.

55. He entered the room with a great flourish and I departed through the side door quietly.

56. As he entered the room I departed.

57. Womens issues will be discussed.

58. I originally enrolled in a writers conference but I later changed my mind and went on a cruise instead.

59. If you have any doubts about being able to attend please let me know.

60. The unit is well designed.

61. A well designed unit won the prize.

62. Forty two people attended the chamber of commerce dinner.

63. She is a highly regarded writer.

64. My husband Peter and I enjoy tennis.

65. My friend Alice is coming for a visit.

66. He grew up in Nashville Tennessee but attended college in the east.

67. Its not easy to put the apostrophe in its place.

68. The Davises house is being remodeled.

69. The company added an employees lunchroom.

70. He was assigned an employees locker.

71. *Everything is easy as long as its happening to someone else.* —Will Rogers

72. *In our country we have three unspeakably precious things freedom of speech freedom of conscience and the prudence never to practice either.* —Mark Twain

73. The company notified its employees.

74. Errors in language are common they happen every day.

75. According to George Burns happiness is having a large loving caring close knit family in another city.

Punctuation and Capitalization Corrected Version:

Shading indicates where punctuation or capitals have been added in the following sentences. If a sentence has no shading, the original version is correct.

51. She is taking a month's vacation.

52. The average urban voter does not appear in the polls.

53. A young, energetic student could handle the assignment.

54. On Friday, I phoned his office and spoke with him.

55. He entered the room with a great flourish, and I departed through the side door quietly.

56. As he entered the room, I departed.

57. Women's issues will be discussed.

58. I originally enrolled in a writers' conference, but I later changed my mind and went on a cruise instead.

59. If you have any doubts about being able to attend, please let me know.

60. The unit is well designed.

61. A well-designed unit won the prize.

62. Forty-two people attended the Chamber of Commerce dinner.

63. She is a highly regarded writer.

64. My husband, Peter, and I enjoy tennis.

65. My friend Alice is coming for a visit.

66. He grew up in Nashville, Tennessee, but attended college in the East.

67. It's not easy to put the apostrophe in its place.

68. The Davises' house is being remodeled.

69. The company added an employees' lunchroom.

70. He was assigned an employee's locker.

71. *Everything is easy as long as it's happening to someone else.* —Will Rogers

72. *In our country, we have three unspeakably precious things: freedom of speech, freedom of conscience, and the prudence never to practice either.* —Mark Twain

73. The company notified its employees.

74. Errors in language are common; they happen every day.

75. According to George Burns, happiness is having a large, loving, caring, close-knit family in another city.

Style:

Edit the following sentences by changing from passive to active voice, correcting misplaced or dangling modifiers, using parallel construction, removing excess words, or eliminating gender bias. *All of the sentences need editing.*

76. Chances are that you have probably heard of our gidget.

77. I refer you back to Paragraph 5 of our proposal.

78. The man who dictates the letter determines its content.

79. The wording of the document is very concise.

80. The research was conducted by a team of biologists and physicists.

81. Every child had learned his lesson.

82. I have discussed how to fill the empty containers with my employees.

83. The new manager, Gabriel Hornblower, and his attractive assistant, Flo Gently, are preparing the final report.

84. Hanging by the fireplace, they saw a picture of a young girl.

85. The supervisor was reprimanded by the Safety Department on two separate occasions.

86. The savvy computer hacker knows his cryptology.

87. There are some circumstances that require new innovative responses.

88. At one a.m. in the morning, the prisoner was granted a temporary reprieve.

89. The reason I am late is because my car wouldn't start.

90. A woman photographer won the prize.

91. The diagram helps you visually see the layout.

92. Select a spokesman for your group.

93. Computer systems have been put to a variety of different applications, with each of which exploiting somewhat different aspects of the computer's capabilities.

    Author's Note: The above sentence was taken from a computer manual that obviously needed editing!

94. Herb Garden and his wife represented the Community Church at the meeting.

95. A well-written letter arouses the reader's interest, contains no errors in punctuation or grammar, and leaving a good impression in the closing lines is important.

96. Everyone who wants to write should be aware of his pet words.

97. "Eat, drink, and being merry" is a cliche.

98. The macaws were observed using binoculars.

99. We will need a dozen people to man the booth.

100. Each applicant should submit his photo.

Style Corrected Version:

The following sentences have been edited to improve the writing style. Where appropriate, crossed-out words indicate changes that have been made.

76. ~~Chances are that~~ You have probably heard of our gidget.
    or Chances are that you have ~~probably~~ heard of our gidget.

77. I refer you ~~back~~ to Paragraph 5 of our proposal.

78. Whoever dictates the letter determines its content.
    or The person who dictates the letter determines its content.

79. The wording of the document is ~~very~~ concise.

80. A team of biologists and physicists conducted the research.

81. All of the children had learned their lessons.

82. I have discussed with my employees how to fill the empty containers.

83. The new manager, Gabriel Hornblower, and his assistant, Flo Gently, are preparing the final report.

84. Hanging by the fireplace was a picture of a young girl.

85. The Safety Department reprimanded the supervisor twice.

86. Savvy computer hackers know their cryptology.

87. ~~There are~~ Some circumstances ~~that~~ require ~~new~~ innovative responses.

88. At one a.m. ~~in the morning~~, the prisoner was granted a ~~temporary~~ reprieve.

89. ~~The reason~~ I am late ~~is~~ because my car wouldn't start.

90. A photographer, Blanche White, won the prize.

91. The diagram helps you ~~visually~~ see the layout.

92. Select a spokesperson for your group.

93. Computer systems have ~~been put to~~ a variety of ~~different~~ applications, ~~with~~ each of which ~~exploiting~~ exploits ~~somewhat~~ different aspects of the computer's capabilities.

94. Herb and Rose Garden represented the Community Church at the meeting.

95. A well-written letter arouses the reader's interest, contains no errors in punctuation or grammar, and leaves a good impression in the closing lines ~~is important.~~

96. Those who want to write should be aware of their pet words.

97. "Eat, drink, and be merry" is a cliche.

98. Using binoculars, we observed the macaws.

99. We will need a dozen people to staff the booth.

100. Submit a photo with your application.

Spelling:

Choose the correctly spelled words in the following sentences.

1. It may come as no (surprise, surprize), but I'd rather take a (Carribean, Caribbean) (cruise, cruse) than (innoculate, inoculate) (dominate, dominant) (monkeys, monkies) in the (Phillippines, Philippines).

2. On April Fool's Day, I (witheld, withheld) my (mortgage, morgage) payment, but the (weird, wierd) loan officer at the bank didn't see the (humor, humer) in my (mischievious, mischievous) little prank.

3. The (incumbant, incumbent) had a (subtle, suttle) (campaign, campane, campain) (stratagy, strategy): (Exaggerate, Exagerate) his own (strengths, strenths), while side-stepping the charges of (harassment, harrassment).

4. You don't have to be a (nuclear, nucular) scientist to see that (flouridation, fluoridation) would make your teeth (flourescent, fluorescent) if you sprayed them with an (aerosol, airosol) of (deisel, diesel) fuel.

5. In a (paralel, parallel) universe, I lived a (desparate, desperate) life as an (unlicenced, unlicensed) (vetinarian, veterinarian) with an (embarassing, embarrassing) habit of (disappearing, disapearing) every (February, Febuary).

6. Let us (procede, proceed) to (excede, exceed) the (permissable, permissible) speed as we (intercede, interceed) on behalf of the (defendant, defendent).

7. Later, we can (develope, develop) a (concensus, consensus) to (reccommend, recommend) a (tariff, tarriff) that will (supercede, supersede) our (maneuver, manuever).

8. He gave me a (memento, momento) of our (liaison, liason, liasion): a (facsimile, facsimilie) of the (indictment, inditement) he had handed down before the court (adjourned, ajourned). He then asked, "Am I being too (foreword, forward, foreward")?

9. If you want your (neice, niece) to be (alright, all right), hand over the (seive, sieve).

10. I don't want to (decieve, deceive) you or appear (sacreligious, sacrilegious), but without the (auxiliary, auxilary) (gauge, guage), this (propeller, propellor) could cause an unfortunate (occurrance, occurrence) for our people in (kahki, khaki, kakhi) and (vice versa, visa versa).

11. (Incidentally, Incidently), an (asterik, asterisk) should (precede, preceed) each (prefered, preferred) item in the left (colum, column).

12. Every (kilowat, kilowatt) of electricity used in producing this (lasar, laser) does (incalcuble, incalculable) good in helping us (fulfill, fullfil) our promise to posterity.

Spelling Corrected Version:

The correct choices (by American English standards) have been made in the following sentences.

1. It may come as no **surprise**, but I'd rather take a **Caribbean cruise** than **inoculate dominant monkeys** in the **Philippines**.

2. On April Fool's Day, I **withheld** my **mortgage** payment, but the **weird** loan officer at the bank didn't see the **humor** in my **mischievous** little prank.

3. The **incumbent** had a **subtle campaign strategy**: **Exaggerate** his own **strengths**, while side-stepping the charges of **harassment**.

4. You don't have to be a **nuclear** scientist to see that **fluoridation** would make your teeth **fluorescent** if you sprayed them with an **aerosol** of **diesel** fuel.

5. In a **parallel** universe, I lived a **desperate** life as an **unlicensed veterinarian** with an **embarrassing** habit of **disappearing** every **February**.

6. Let us **proceed** to **exceed** the **permissible** speed as we **intercede** on behalf of the **defendant**.

7. Later, we can **develop** a **consensus** to **recommend** a **tariff** that will **supersede** our **maneuver**.

8. He gave me a **memento** of our **liaison**: a **facsimile** of the **indictment** he had handed down before the court **adjourned**. He then asked, "Am I being too **forward**?"

9. If you want your **niece** to be **all right**, hand over the **sieve**.

10. I don't want to **deceive** you or appear **sacrilegious**, but without the **auxiliary gauge**, this **propeller** could cause an unfortunate **occurrence** for our people in **khaki** and **vice versa**.

11. **Incidentally**, an **asterisk** should **precede** each **preferred** item in the left **column**.

12. Every **kilowatt** of electricity used in producing this **laser** does **incalculable** good in helping us **fulfill** our promise to posterity.

13. The (vicious, viscious) (committee, comittee) members decided to pursue (their, there, they're) objectives by filing a (greivance, grievance, grievence) and requesting a (waiver, waver) of the (remittance, remittence, remitance).

14. (Basically, Basicly), the (cencus, census) showed no (consistancy, consistency) among the (independant, independent) variables, even when calculated in the (binary, binery) mode.

15. (Tucson's, Tuscon's) infamous (tobacco, tabacco) (theif, thief) turned out to be a (physician, physicion) with a (preferance, preference) for a (spoonful, spoonfull) of (inflamation, inflammation). The (villain, villian) experienced a (religous, religious) conversion after a (breif, brief) stay in prison.

16. His misuse of (grammar, grammer) and his (perrennial, perennial) (mispelling, misspelling) of (certain, certian) (relevant, relevent) words put him in the (catagory, category) of friends who will (definately, definitely) (receive, recieve) a (dictionery, dictionary) from me at the next appropriate (ocassion, occasion).

17. You have each been (alloted, allotted) three (baloons, balloons) and (miscellanious, miscellaneous) (peices, pieces) of (jewelry, jewellery), which I (gaurantee, guarantee) you will find (indispensible, indispensable) in the (arctic, artic).

18. With the city under (seige, siege), the (leutenant, lieutenant) made a (judgment, judgement) call and increased (survailance, surveilllance) with a (vengeance, vengence).

19. As an (acessory, accessory) to the crime, I found a (battalion, battallion) of (blatant, blatent) do-gooders attempting to appeal to my (consience, conscience).

20. She (acknowleged, acknowledged) his (presence, presance) as he stood on the (threshold, threshhold) looking (exausted, exhausted), but she refused to (yeild, yield) the (Portugese, Portuguese) (miniture, miniature) that was (liable, lible) to put her in (jeopardy, jepardy).

21. (Your, you're) (unneccessary, unnecessary) (repetition, repitition) of (mathmatical, mathematical) equations has the (predictible, predictable) (affect, effect) of increasing (aspirin, asprin) (usage, useage) and acting as a (deterrent, deterrant) to your success in (busness, business).

22. (Apropo, Apropos) your (acquittal, aquittal), I'd like to (acommodate, accommodate, accomodate) your request to use the (apparatus, aparatus), but your (alottment, allotment) of time has been (exceded, exceeded).

23. At the (cemetary, cemetery, sematary), the (concensus, consensus) of the (caucus, caucas) was that only the (competant, competent) should be allowed to make a (committment, commitment) to a (particular, particuler) (calender, calander, calendar) date

13. The **vicious committee** members decided to pursue **their** objectives by filing a **grievance** and requesting a **waiver** of the **remittance**.

14. **Basically**, the **census** showed no **consistency** among the **independent** variables, even when calculated in the **binary** mode.

15. **Tucson's** infamous **tobacco thief** turned out to be a **physician** with a **preference** for a **spoonful** of **inflammation**. The **villain** experienced a **religious** conversion after a **brief** stay in prison.

16. His misuse of **grammar** and his **perennial misspelling** of **certain relevant** words put him in the **category** of friends who will **definitely receive** a **dictionary** from me at the next appropriate **occasion**.

17. You have each been **allotted** three **balloons** and **miscellaneous pieces** of **jewelry**, which I **guarantee** you will find **indispensable** in the **arctic**.

18. With the city under **siege**, the **lieutenant** made a **judgment** call and increased **surveillance** with a **vengeance**.

19. As an **accessory** to the crime, I found a **battalion** of **blatant** do-gooders attempting to appeal to my **conscience**.

20. She **acknowledged** his **presence** as he stood on the **threshold** looking **exhausted**, but she refused to **yield** the **Portuguese miniature** that was **liable** to put her in **jeopardy**.

21. **Your unnecessary repetition** of **mathematical** equations has the **predictable effect** of increasing **aspirin usage** and acting as a **deterrent** to your success in **business**.

22. **Apropos** your **acquittal**, I'd like to **accommodate** your request to use the **apparatus**, but your **allotment** of time has been **exceeded**.

23. At the **cemetery**, the **consensus** of the **caucus** was that only the **competent** should be allowed to make a **commitment** to a **particular calendar** date.

24. Once inside the (vacume, vacuum) chamber, (rhythm, rythm) becomes (irrelevent, irrelevant), but you will be (seized, siezed) by an (ecstacy, ecstasy) (similiar, similar) to chocolate-induced (euphoria, uphoria).

25. Living under a (seperate, separate) (paradime, paradigm), we had the (priviledge, privilege) of (publically, publicly) (seceeding, seceding), but our (hypocricy, hypocrisy) was immediately (discernable, discernible).

26. She had always believed in (maintainance, maintenance) and kept her house (immaculate, imacculate), but she (inadvertantly, inadvertently) developed an (irresistable, irresistible) urge to (accummulate, accumulate) (paraphenalia, paraphernalia).

27. With a (flourish, fluorish), she stepped on the (accelerater, accelerator) (pedal, petal, peddle) and took off like a (missile, missal, misile, mistle) through the open (prarie, prairie) headed for (Pitsburg, Pittsburgh), calling back in her (exilaration, exhilaration), "Your (milage, mileage) may vary!"

28. One of my (antecedants, antecedents) (exibited, exhibited) a (tendancy, tendency) to (pedal, petal, peddle) software by claiming, "My computer has more (kilobites, kilobytes) of memory than yours!"

29. His basic (tenant, tenet) was to settle all disputes between landlords and (tenants, tenets) quickly.

30. The book's (foreward, forward, foreword) (homed, honed) in on the need for catching (mispelled, misspelled) words

24. Once inside the **vacuum** chamber, **rhythm** becomes **irrelevant**, but you will be **seized** by an **ecstasy similar** to chocolate-induced **euphoria**.

25. Living under a **separate paradigm**, we had the **privilege** of **publicly seceding**, but our **hypocrisy** was immediately **discernible**.

26. She had always believed in **maintenance** and kept her house **immaculate**, but she **inadvertently** developed an **irresistible** urge to **accumulate paraphernalia**.

27. With a **flourish**, she stepped on the **accelerator pedal** and took off like a **missile** through the open **prairie** headed for **Pittsburgh**, calling back in her **exhilaration**, "Your **mileage** may vary!"

28. One of my **antecedents exhibited** a **tendency** to **peddle** software by claiming, "My computer has more **kilobytes** of memory than yours!"

29. His basic **tenet** was to settle all disputes between landlords and **tenants** quickly.

30. The book's **foreword homed** in on the need for catching **misspelled** words.

Resources for the Letter Writer

Letter Writing

Cool, Lisa, *How to Write Irresistible Query Letters*, Cincinnati, OH: Writer's Digest Books, 1990.

DeVries, Mary A., *Internationally Yours: Writing and Communicating Successfully in Today's Global Marketplace*, Boston: Houghton-Mifflin Co., 1994.

DeVries, Mary A., *The New American Handbook of Letter Writing and Other Forms of Correspondence*, New York: Random House Value, 1993.

Frailey, L. E., *Handbook of Business Letters, 3rd Ed.*, Englewood Cliffs, NJ: Prentice-Hall, Inc., 1989.

Heller, Bernard, *The 100 Most Difficult Business Letters You'll Ever Have to Write, Fax, or E-Mail*, New York: HarperBusiness, 1994.

Merriam-Webster's Secretarial Handbook, 3rd Ed., Springfield, MA: Merriam-Webster, Inc., 1993.

Meyer, Harold E., *Lifetime Encyclopedia of Letters*, Englewood Cliffs, NJ: Prentice-Hall, Inc., 1992.

Dictionaries

American Heritage Dictionary of the English Language, Boston, MA: Houghton-Mifflin Co.

Concise Oxford Dictionary of Current English, London: Oxford University Press.

Dictionary of Modern English Usage, Henry W. Fowler, London: Oxford University Press.

Funk & Wagnall's New Comprehensive Dictionary of the English Language, New York: HarperCollins.

Merriam-Webster's Collegiate Dictionary, Springfield, MA: Merriam- Webster, Inc.

Random House College Dictionary, New York: Random House Inc.

Random House Unabridged Dictionary, New York: Random House Inc.

Roget's International Thesaurus, New York: HarperCollins.

Webster's Third New International Dictionary (unabridged), Springfield, MA: Merriam-Webster, Inc.

Etiquette

Axtell, Robert E., ed., *Do's and Taboos Around the World*, 2nd Ed., New York: John Wiley, 1990.

Phillips, Linda, *Concise Guide to Executive Etiquette*, Garden City, NY: Doubleday, 1990.

Post, Elizabeth L., *Emily Post on Business Etiquette*, New York: HarperCollins, 1990.

Bias-Free Writing

Maggio, Rosalie, *Nonsexist Word Finder: A Dictionary of Gender-Free Usage*, Phoenix, AZ: Oryx Press, 1987.

Miller, Casey, and Kate Swift, *The Handbook of Nonsexist Writing*, New York: HarperCollins, 1988.

Pickens, Judy E., ed., *Without Bias: A Guidebook for Nondiscriminatory Communication*, 2nd Ed., New York: John Wiley & Sons, 1982.

Resumes and Career-related

Asher, Donald, *The Foolproof Job-Search Workbook*, Berkeley, CA: Ten Speed Press, 1995.

Asher, Donald, *The Overnight Job Change Letter*, Berkeley, CA: Ten Speed Press, 1994.

Bolles, Richard Nelson, *What Color Is Your Parachute? A Practical Manual for Job-Hunters and Career-Changers*, Berkeley, CA: Ten Speed Press, (current edition).

Fox, Marcia R., *Put Your Degree to Work, 2nd Ed.*, New York: W. W. Norton & Co., Inc., 1988.

Hansen, Katharine, and Randall Hansen, *Dynamic Cover Letters*, Berkeley, CA: Ten Speed Press, 1995.

Medley, H. Anthony, *Sweaty Palms: The Neglected Art of Being Interviewed (rev.)*, Berkeley, CA: Ten Speed Press, 1992.

Parker, Yana, *Blue Collar and Beyond: Resumes for Skilled Trades and Services*, Berkeley, CA: Ten Speed Press, 1995.

Parker, Yana, *Damn Good Resume Guide, (rev.)*, Berkeley, CA: Ten Speed Press, 1989.

Writing Aids

Chicago Manual of Style, The, 14th ed., Chicago: University of Chicago Press, 1993.

Drummond, Val, *Grammar for Grownups: A Guide to Grammar & Usage for Everyone Who Has to Put Words on Paper Effectively*, New York: Harper-Perennial, 1993.

Dusseau, John L., *Bugaboos, Chimeras, and Achilles' Heels: 10,001 Difficult Words and How to Use Them*, Englewood Cliffs, NJ: Prentice Hall, Inc., 1993.

Murray, Donald, *Writing for Your Readers: Notes on the Writer's Craft from the Boston Globe, 2nd ed.*, Chester, CT: Globe Pequot, 1992.

Parker, Roger C., *Looking Good in Print, 2nd ed.*, Alexandria, VA: Tools of the Trade, 1992.

Sabin, William A., *The Gregg Reference Manual, 7th ed.*, Glencoe, IL: Gregg Division/McGraw-Hill Book Co., 1992.

Shaw, Harry, *Errors in English and Ways to Correct Them*, New York: Harper-Perennial, 1993.

Tarshis, Barry, *Grammar for Smart People: Your User-Friendly Guide to Speaking and Writing Better English*, New York: Pocket Books, 1992.

Venolia, Jan, *Rewrite Right! How to Revise Your Way to Better Writing*, Berkeley, CA: Ten Speed Press, 1987.

Venolia, Jan, *Write Right! A Desktop Digest of Punctuation, Grammar & Style, 3rd ed.*, Berkeley, CA: Ten Speed Press, 1995.

U. S. Postal Service Publications:

Domestic Mail Manual

Domestic Postage Rates, Fees, and Information

International Mail Manual

International Postage Rates and Fees

National ZIP Code Directory

Postal Addressing Standards

> (available through the National Address Information Center, Memphis, TN, 1-800-238-3150)

Index

A

Abbreviations, 59, 65, 68, 77, 79, 156-160
Abstractions, 10-11
Active voice, 22
Address
   forms of, 161-167
   inside, 62-63
   outside, 77-80
   overseas, 80
AIDA, 36
Appendixes, 151-181
Attention line, 65-66, 79

B

Bibliography, 182
Block Letter format, 53
Brevity, 18-21, 41
Business letters
   elements of, 59-77
   samples of, 52-57, 97-132

C

Clarity, 6-17
Cliches, 8, 18, 43
Closing paragraphs, 42-43
Complimentary close, 70-71, 137
Conciseness, 18-21
Concrete vs. abstract, 10-11
Continuation pages, 69-70
Copy Notation, 76-77

D, E

Date, 48-49, 59-60
Dictionary, usefulness of, 7, 13
Distribution of copies, 76-77
E-mail, 27-28
Emphasis, 23-24, 27
Enclosure Notation, 75-76
Envelopes, 77-80

F

Fax Transmittal form, 58
Fog, 6

Format, business letter, 50-57
   Block, 53
   Memorandum, 57
   Modified Block, 54
   Modified Semiblock, 55
   Official, 56
   Simplified, 52
Format, personal letter, 137
Forms of address, 161-167

H, I, J

Hackneyed expressions, 8-10, 154-155
Hyphenation, 68-69
Identification line, 75
Informal terminology, 13
Inside address, 62-63
Itemizing, 24
Jargon, 8-10, 155-157
Job Titles and Descriptions, 93-94

L

Letters
   advantages of, 2
   closing of, 42-43
   composing, 31-45
   effective, 5
   length of, 41
   more than one page, 69-70
   opening of, 38-40
   tone of, 37-38
Letter formulas, 36
Letter-writing style, 5-28

M

Mailing notations, 60-61
Margins, 48-49
Memorandum, 57, 86
Misplaced words, 17-18
Modified Block Letter, 54
Modified Semiblock Letter, 55
Modifier
   dangling, 17-18

M, *cont'd*
  misplaced, 17-18
  overused, 19-21
  squinting, 17

N
Names
  couples', 88-89
  hyphenated, 89
  in inside address, 64-65
Numbered material, 24, 69
Numbers, in addresses, 63

O
Official Letter format, 56
On-Arrival Notations, 61
Opening paragraphs, 38-40
Organization, 31-35
Outlining, 32-35
Outside address, 77-80
Overseas Addresses, 80

P
Padding, 18-21, 41
Paragraph
  closing, 42-43
  opening, 38-40
  topic sentence, 26
  unified impression, 27
Parallel form, 24
Passive voice, 22
Personal letters, 135-151
Post office box, 63
Postscript, 77
Proofreading, 44-45
Punctuation in letters, 49-50

Q, R
Quizzes
  grammar & usage, 168-171
  punctuation & capitalization, 172-173
  spelling, 176-181
  style, 174-175
Reader, visualizing, 36-37
Reference Line, 60
Resources for the Letter Writer, 182-184
Revising, 43-44

S
Salutation, 66, 84-89
Sample letters
  business, 52-57, 97-132
  job-related, 123-132
  personal, 135-151
Second sheets, 69-70
Sentences
  length of, 25
  monotonous, 26
  topic, 26
Sexist terms, avoiding, 83-94
Signature, 71-75
Simplified Letter format, 52, 87
Special Mailing Notations, 60-61
Spelling
  preferred, 7-8
  quiz, 176-181
Stationery, 48-49
Style, 5-28
Subject line, 67-68

T, V
Titles, 64-65, 84-89
Tone, 37-38
Vagueness, 5, 10-11
Verbs, action, 12-13, 154
Voice
  active, 22
  passive, 22

W, Z
Wordiness, 18-21
Words, 7-18
  as tools, 7
  commonly misused, 13-14
  concrete, 10-11
  correct, 13-14
  division of, 68-69
  familiar, 12-13
  misplaced, 17-18
  short, 12-13
  shortened, 13
  stilted, 8-10, 154-155
  vague, 6, 10-11
  vigorous, 11-12
ZIP Code, 63, 78-79, 156